KU-680-891

Performance assessment in academic libraries

1255578

STEVE MORGAN

Performance assessment in academic libraries

MANSELL

First published 1995 by
Mansell Publishing Limited, *A Cassell imprint*
Wellington House, 125 Strand, London WC2R 0BB, England
215 Park Avenue South, New York, New York 10003, USA

© Steve Morgan, Mike Heery, Julie Parry and Geoffrey Ford 1995

All rights reserved. No part of this publication may be reproduced or transmitted in any
form or by any means, electronic or mechanical, including photocopy, recording or any
information storage or retrieval system, without permission in writing from the
Publishers or their appointed agents.

British Library Cataloguing-in-Publication Data

Morgan, Steve
　　Performance Assessment in Academic Libraries
　　I.　Title
　　027.7

　　　ISBN 0-7201-2188-4

Library of Congress Cataloging-in-Publication Data

Morgan, Steve
　　Performance assessment in academic libraries/Steve Morgan.
　　　p.　　cm.
　　Includes bibliographical references and index.
　　ISBN 0-7201-2188-4　:　$70.00
　　1.　Academic libraries--Evaluation.　　I.　Title.
　　2675.U5M64　1995　　　　　　　　　　　　　94-45209
　　027.7--dc20　　　　　　　　　　　　　　　　　CIP

Typeset by Action Typesetting Limited, Gloucester

Printed and bound in Great Britain by Biddles Ltd, Guildford & Kings Lynn

Contents

List of illustrations

Figures

Tables

List of appendices

Appendices III–V are taken from Van House *et al.* (1990) with permission to photocopy.

Abbreviations

BTEC	Business and Technician Education Council
BNBRF	British National Bibliography Research Fund
CCTV	Closed circuit television
CD-ROM	Compact Disk-Read Only Memory
CNAA	Council for National Academic Awards
COFHE	Council of Further and Higher Education
COLRiC	Council for Learning Resources in Colleges
COPOL	Council of Polytechnic Librarians
CVCP	Committee of Vice Chancellors and Principals
FE	Further education
FEFC	Further Education Funding Council
FTE	Full-time equivalent
GCSE	General Certificate of Secondary Education
GNVQ	General National Vocational Qualification
HEFCE	Higher Education Funding Council for England
HEQC	Higher Education Quality Council
IFLA	International Federation of Library Associations
JANET	Joint Academic Network
MBO	Management by objectives
MIS	Management information systems
MRAP	Management review and analysis programme
NHS	National Health Service
OPACs	Online Public Access Catalogues
PBB	Priority based budgeting
PPBS	Programme planning budgeting system
SCONUL	Standing Conference of National and University Libraries
SUPERJANET	An Improved/Enhanced Joint Academic Network
TQM	Total quality management
ZBBS	Zero-based budgeting system

Preface

If I were asked to categorize this book, I would place it firmly in the textbook genre. However, things are never as clear-cut as they seem. Admittedly, for the library manager, practitioner or student in the further and higher education sectors there are stopping-off points (extensive references and sections of further reading). These are meant to supplement and build upon the overview of performance assessment detailed in the ten chapters. But since any kind of rigorous evaluation normally entails some activity, you will find pieces of advice and hints scattered throughout the text (especially in Chapter 9). But this does not make it a 'how-to-do' book.

This book is more concerned with the qualitative assessment of front-line reader services and staff (Chapters 5–8) and with exploring the perspectives of the various constituents – the managers, the users and the library staff (Chapters 2–4). It does not pretend to be comprehensive. The minutiae of performance indicator construction and the cost implications, for example, are really only touched upon. The intention is to provide a snapshot of performance assessment in cademic libraries in these turbulent times and to stimulate interest in what is undoubtedly one of those management concepts that is here to stay.

As this book is about to go to print, a potentially important document (Joint Funding Councils, 1995) has been put out for consultation. Although referred to briefly in Chapter 10, this proposed framework for assessing academic library services has appeared too late for detailed consideration here.

I would like to offer my sincere thanks to three colleagues in particular who not only sacrificed precious time to devote to (more) writing but were also a source of encouragement – both verbal and by example. Thanks to Mike Heery, Julie Parry and Geoffrey Ford for their valuable contributions in the form of Chapters 3, 8 and 10 respectively.

Steve Morgan
Newport, Gwent
April 1995

CHAPTER ONE

Performance assessment: an introduction

Performance indicators are a means of assisting responsible management to make efficient and effective decisions. They are not, however, a mechanical substitute for good judgement, political wisdom or leadership.

(Jackson, 1988, p.15)

The issues covered in this chapter are:

- the nature of performance assessment;
- the reasons for performance assessment;
- some influential publications;
- the influence of the private sector.

The idea of assessing the performance of an organization has been a central tenet of management thinking for a number of years. Some managers would have happily settled for making a profit – however large or small. Indeed, the security of the jobs of many people would be dependent on it. Such a criterion for assessment may be considered rather crude in the late twentieth century particularly with the complex nature of some of the world's multinational organizations. Those that operate in the public services sector will have a different set of criteria and methods with which to assess performance. These 'not-for-profit' organizations will inevitably pursue objectives and follow funding arrangements which differ from those in the private sector. This is developed further later in this chapter.

Having accepted that organizations, regardless of their environment or the type of business in which they operate, have procedures which, to a greater or lesser extent, assess how well or how badly they are performing, we need to be clear about:

- what performance assessment is;
- why performance assessment is necessary;
- how performance is assessed.

In order to place the assessment of performance into context we should also consider:

- recent publications which have summarized or have had some influence on performance assessment thinking;
- how assessment of performance in the public sector is different from, and has been influenced by, that of the private sector.

The whole area of judging the quality and effectiveness of a public service such as an academic library is intrinsically complex (see Figure 1.1). Whilst the inputs, processes and outputs of a service can usually be measured or assessed, the outcome (the long-term impact of the input/process) becomes problematic. An example in a library context would be as follows: an information skills programme could consist of a series of seminars or workshops using a variety of learning support aids. The input into the programme is in terms of staff time and resources, the process consists of the teaching/learning experience of the participants, the output may be a group of satisfied and informed students better able to retrieve information from the library. However, what benefits have accrued from the series of seminars that have a direct bearing on the students' course results? Such wider and long-term outcomes are known as higher order effects. This example demonstrates the difficulty of assessing the outcome or impact of an educational interaction which forms part of a more extensive programme of study. One has to isolate the effects of the service from all the other influences on the 'target' population.

WHAT IS PERFORMANCE ASSESSMENT?

Performance assessment is simply a way of helping us to find out how good or bad service provision is; it relates performance to objectives. The service may be assessed in relation to itself, called a time series (how effective was the readers' enquiry service this year as compared with last?) or indeed a comparison may be made with other similar services (the library spend per student across two or three different libraries). This latter exercise is one of a number of attempts in recent years to make use of league tables for comparative purposes, particularly in the education sector. Such

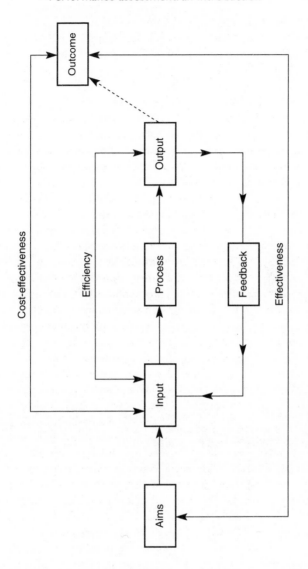

Figure 1.1. Systems model of performance assessment.

comparisons have inherent dangers, e.g. failure to compare like with like, oversimplification etc.

Performance may also be assessed against preset norms or standards (Kania, 1988; McElroy, 1989). However, such standards must be regularly updated to take account of changing circumstances in the academic sector.

Assessment may be carried out on two levels – macro and micro. At the macro level the performance capability of the whole service would be under consideration – a holistic view. Research by McDonald and Micikas (1994) is a recent example of such holism using an organizational effectiveness model. Such an assessment would inevitably comprise a combination of micro level evaluations, including those services considered in Chapters 5–7, to make up a more three-dimensional picture. Lancaster (1993) follows this approach in assessing the effectiveness of various library facets independently and building up a composite picture. This represents the view favoured in this book.

TERMINOLOGY

It has been acknowledged by a number of commentators (MacDougall, 1991) that the terminology which surrounds the evaluation of an academic library service can be rather misleading. It would be beneficial to clarify my interpretation of these terms at this fairly early stage. For further explanation of terminology Ford (1989) and Ford and MacDougall (1992) are particularly helpful.

Evaluation

McClure (1985, p.195) defines evaluation as:

a systematic process which assesses the efficiency and effectiveness of certain activities and offers a value judgement of their value in terms of some criteria (such as goals and objectives).

Evaluation represents a practical activity whose results may well inform the managerial decision-making process. It is not a sterile intellectual exercise. One method of evaluation is through the use of performance indicators (Abbott, 1994). Cronin (1982) provides an excellent overview of evaluation in the general library context.

Assessment

The term tends to be used in the UK, whereas the term 'evaluation' would be used in the US. For the purposes of judging the performance of academic libraries and for convenience sake in this book both terms may be deemed as synonymous. Indeed, 'assess' is included in the (Concise Oxford) dictionary definition of 'evaluate'.

Inputs

The inputs into an academic library service consist primarily of financial resources which are translated secondarily into appropriate staffing, collections of books and periodicals, electronic databases and other physical plant. Such inputs would not be evaluated per se but in terms of the role played by them in the library context. For example, the library's collection (input) would be evaluated in terms of satisfying the demands placed upon it (output). These items are tangible and easily quantifiable in terms of costs and numbers.

Outputs

The outputs from an academic library represent the services provided by that library, for example the number of reference enquiries accurately answered, the number of user education sessions successfully delivered, the success in providing appropriate textbooks to support a student project. Some outputs may be less tangible than inputs but more tangible than outcomes, and their assessment should be qualitative in nature (Van House, 1989).

Outcomes or Impacts

As previously suggested, outcomes are often the most difficult indicators to assess. Outcomes represent the impact which the outputs of a service have on a target population. For example, provision of an enquiry service represents one output from an academic library; for a particular user the outcome of a reference enquiry would be the successful retrieval of a name, address, telephone number from which to obtain vital information for an assignment. The measurement of the actual impact of academic libraries, that is, how students' use of libraries affects their academic performance, is notoriously difficult (Powell, 1992).

Performance Measures

Dalton (1988, p.31) describes performance measures as 'precise and quantifiable indicators which serve as a gauge for the overall performance of a service, that is, the measures identify the amount of services (quantity) and their level of effectiveness (quality)'.

Examples of such measures include bookfund per FTE (full time equivalent), interlibrary loan turnaround time, study space per FTE etc. Often the use of indicators is viewed as one method of measuring performance but, as Dalton indicates, there is some overlap.

Economy

Economy may be described as the purchasing of inputs – staff, collections etc. – of the appropriate quality and quantity for the lowest possible cost. An example of uneconomical behaviour would be overstaffing. Total library space per FTE student and total spend per FTE student are examples of economy indicators.

Efficiency

Efficiency is considered as the relationship between the outputs of the library service and the resources required to provide them, that is, the ratio of input to output. The smaller the ratio, the more output for input and the more efficient the library. This ratio may be improved by either increasing output whilst keeping inputs constant or alternatively decreasing inputs whilst outputs remain constant. Cost per loan and documents delivered per FTE number of library staff are examples of efficiency indicators.

Effectiveness

Effectiveness which may be seen as an outward-looking measure (as opposed to efficiency which is more an inward-looking measure) is the degree to which the library is achieving its aims and objectives including ensuring that its policy aims are being met. Effectiveness is concerned with outcomes or impacts – the effects of the service on users. Since effectiveness is assessed against a baseline (the various aims and objectives of the library service), it is imperative that the aims and objectives are sufficiently wide or stretching to be fully appropriate. One way of measuring performance effectiveness is to gauge satisfaction levels of users with elements of the service or the service as a whole. This may be carried out directly, for example by checking the availability of books and periodicals, or indirectly by asking users for their views.

Cost-effectiveness

Cost-effectiveness is an indicator which shows the costs to the library of achieving its aims and objectives. Examples of such measures would include cost per document supplied, cost per information unit supplied, cost per study hour. The cost-effectiveness of a service may be improved by keeping costs at a constant level whilst increasing effectiveness. Similarly, it may be achieved by maintaining the level of effectiveness whilst reducing the costs incurred in providing the service.

Equity

Some commentators (Bovaird et al., 1988; Open University, 1991) have included equity as a criterion considered to be particularly pertinent in the public service sector. Equity may be defined in terms of justice and fairness – the equal treatment of individuals and groups in similar situations. For example, a student at an academic library enquiry point is entitled to receive as effective a service regardless of the librarian who is on duty at the time.

WHY IS PERFORMANCE ASSESSED?

Up to the mid-1970s increasing inputs was seen as a desirable option to improve library performance. Such a view was shared by governments and service providers. During the 1980s an increasing amount of literature appeared on the subject of performance assessment within the public service sector (see Further Reading). Much of the interest concentrated on controlling the growth of inputs (economy) and relating them more closely to outputs (efficiency). More recently the emphasis has shifted to the assessment of the outputs (effectiveness) of services including the 'quality' debate (Brophy et al., 1993; Ellis and Norton, 1993; Winkworth, 1993) and the continued rise of charterism. This is further developed in the next chapter. Such a change of emphasis has necessitated that the focus of attention falls on the users or consumers of the services in question.

A variety of reasons may be put forward for this increasing interest in public sector performance assessment, and in academic libraries in particular. Some are driven by forces external to the library, others are driven by internal forces. The external pressures come from academic managers within higher education institutions who recognize that the library service alongside other faculties, departments and support services has to justify its existence. Libraries – academic or otherwise – have no divine right to receive funding because they are perceived as intrinsically 'good'. Those days are long gone. The library has to be seen to demonstrate a commitment to efficiency and effectiveness, thereby providing evidence of 'good' management practices. Parent organizations are concerned – quite rightly – about rising costs in central and support services including administration and computing services, as well as in the academic departments.

Internally, academic libraries have become larger and more complex organizations which therefore require objective standardized data for management decision making. In many instances libraries form part of a multi-site operation, in other cases libraries and computing services have converged under one organizational umbrella. Increasing demands on the service from ever more computer-literate and sophisticated users (in ever greater numbers) have put additional pressure on library managers to ensure that their needs are satisfied. Performance assessment is necessary to flag up problem areas so that improvements may be planned on a rational basis. This point is implied in the quotation at the start of the chapter and in the Follett Report: 'performance indicators are intended to prompt questions as much as provide answers' (Joint Funding Councils' Libraries Review Group, 1993, p.32). Library managers are being forced to disperse inadequate resources over an increasing range of functions and specialist activities. In many cases the library is unable to maintain the desired or expected level of service.

The purposes for which performance assessment is required differ. At the institutional level it may assist the library manager to obtain and allocate resources, defend the library against budget reductions and make explicit the effects of policy changes. At the service level the library manager is able to gauge the success of innovations or establish benchmarks to show current levels (for later comparison). Chapter 4 provides a snapshot of the nature and extent of performance assessment activity taking place in the early 1990s in academic libraries in both the further and higher education sectors.

Library managers may also wish to make comparisons across different libraries. This may be problematic since incomparable data collection results in incomparable data. The number of measures to be used and the different ways in which libraries operate would ensure that comparability across libraries or indeed library units could prove an unreliable exercise. For example, it may simply be the case that one library is very busy whilst another is rather slack at the time of comparison.

HOW IS PERFORMANCE ASSESSED?

The assessment of a library service's performance may be subjective, objective or a combination of the two. Subjective assessment is based on people's opinions or views. These can be valuable since it is important for library managers to have access to users' feelings about the service or a particular aspect of it. Objective assessment, on the other hand, requires criteria and procedures the results of which should be quantifiable. The development of ever more sophisticated automated library systems has ensured that large amounts of data are available for performance assessment and management decision-making purposes. Such systems also can obviate the need for sampling since appropriate data may be gathered as a continuous byproduct of the operation of the system, for example identification of the most heavily used titles, subject distribution, rates of obsolescence etc.

Just as there is no one single criterion for assessing performance so there is not one methodological technique that can be deployed. Often assessment is carried out in various aspects of a service so that different methods may be appropriate for different aspects, for example the enquiry service may be evaluated by an observer and a checklist, failure rates at the book shelves may be evaluated by the completion of forms by users, an information skills session may be evaluated through a follow-up questionnaire.

Extensive use has been made of user surveys (Harris, 1991) representing subjective assessment. These have been criticized by Powell (1988) amongst others because of the unreliability and variable expectations of user opinions. All commentators emphasize that a wide range of techniques should be deployed including a variety of types of survey, for example checklists, interviews, questionnaires, simulations. Line and Stone (1982) provide an excellent resumé for gaining an understanding of the range of techniques available. Chapter 9 concentrates on the survey as the major methodological tool.

INFLUENTIAL PUBLICATIONS

For comprehensive coverage of the literature on performance assessment readers should refer to the following: Evans *et al.* (1972), Reynolds (1970), Goodall (1988), McLean and Wilde (1991), Blagden and Harrington (1990). Lancaster's (1993) formidable list of references (over 400) reflects the current picture of performance assessment and covers all types of libraries. This publication is considered in greater detail below. Other publications which deal with the practicalities of performance indicators are those by Abbott (1994) and Cotta-Schonberg and Line (1994). However, in truth, few successful attempts at implementing comprehensive programmes are recorded.

Much of the early work on the topic revolved around quantitative issues including costs, with an emphasis on measuring inputs into the library system. Morse (1968), Wessel (1968) and Orr (1973) are excellent examples of this approach. There is, however, little evidence that the methods outlined in these works have been applied operationally.

Since those initial quantitative forays there have been a number of publications which have impacted on the evaluation of academic library services. Publications which provide either historical or contemporary assistance in informing the performance assessment debate will be pointed out at appropriate points in the text. The following represent three particularly influential publications on the subject. They are: Kantor (1984), Van House *et al.* (1990) and Lancaster (1993).

Kantor, P. B. *Objective performance measures for academic and research libraries*

The measures outlined in this seminal work are intended to be practical and replicated (copious proforma sheets are provided at the back). Specific measures were tested in five US academic libraries: availability and accessibility of library materials, and delay analysis of interlibrary loan activities. Within this manual the emphasis is placed upon the use of objective measures of service quality to aid the management decision making process. The author stresses the resource implications of any performance measurement exercises – planning, execution, analysis, dissemination. The end product must be worth the input of staff time, a point made frequently in Morgan's (1993) survey. Those institutions which run

Library and Information courses may be better served since they can deploy students as part of their project/dissertation work.

The author recommends stem and leaf analysis for measuring the accessibility of books. Accessibility represents a measure of the amount of effort required to look up, retrieve and check out materials in the collection. The analysis involves completing time sheets to measure, in this example, the process from searching the library catalogue, through finding the book and taking it to the issue desk, to completing the transaction. Such methods of measurement may be replicated in other library services, for example interlibrary loans, finding periodicals in stacks, book acquisition and throughput.

Availability represents a measure of the extent to which user needs for specific documents are promptly satisfied. The availability ratio is obtained by using branch analysis on a minimum of 400 specific document requests. Such analysis will inevitably highlight areas of concern, for example ineffective use of the library catalogue, implications for collection development, difficulty in finding material on the shelves etc.

Availability and accessibility are considered further in Chapter 5.

This publication represents a good example in terms of:

- practicality;
- replication of methods;
- pertinence;
- tried and tested methods.

Van House, N. *et al. Measuring academic library performance: a practical approach*
As the title suggests, this publication advocates a hands-on approach to assessment. This approach is underlined by the formidable array of questionnaires and checklists available for photocopying (see Appendices III–V) and also the worked examples scattered throughout the text. Emphasis is placed on the evaluation of services provided for the library's clientele – the so-called front-line services. Measurement of internal library processes is excluded (unlike in the Kantor publication).

Although coverage of services is fairly comprehensive (with the exception of user education), the authors stress that libraries need to select the measures which suit their own particular needs at particular times. It is hoped that, by employing a suitable raft of measures, a meaningful assessment of the library's services will result.

Following discussion of measurement and user surveys, Van House and her colleagues concentrate on fifteen measures covering four categories of academic library use – general satisfaction, materials availability and use, facilities and library use, information services. Each of the measures consists of a standard format including definition, background, data collection and analysis, discussion and further suggestions.

This publication represents a good example in terms of:

- practicality;
- service-oriented measures;
- replication of methods;
- specific focus on academic libraries.

Lancaster, F.W. *If you want to evaluate your library...*
This expanded edition has updated each of its chapters and also included a welcome chapter 'Evaluation of bibliographic instruction'. As indicated in the survey in Chapter 4, only a minority of libraries assessed the performance of their user education and enquiry/reference services. It is gratifying therefore to see wide coverage of both areas in this publication. The particular difficulties relating to these information services, for example assessment of quality, measurement of attitudes/satisfaction levels, long-term effectiveness, are addressed only patchily. The reasons are plain – there are no easy solutions to these issues.

The sixteen chapters are divided into three sections – Document Delivery Services, Reference Services, Other Aspects, the first being by far the most detailed. Lancaster is very strong on the evaluation of library collections, both books and periodicals, including Kantor's availability and accessibility. The author also succeeds in incorporating the evaluation of electronic services including OPACs, database searching and CD-ROMs. The third section concentrates on the financial aspects of performance assessment which are excluded from the previous two publications.

This publication represents a good example in terms of:

- practicality;
- extensive use of empirical evidence;
- comprehensive coverage.

A combination of these three publications would provide the library manager with a pragmatic and thoroughly researched collection of performance assessment criteria. Whilst a rich armoury of assessment criteria exists, it is their selection, combination and integration which will paint the required performance picture. This could provide the means to support the decision-making process for improving services. Performance assessment is not an end in itself. The library manager is the final arbiter: do the results from the selected criteria form a representative view of the library's performance at that point in time? This is very much the approach of SCONUL in Chapter 10. In the end judgement must necessarily be a subjective one given the difficulties of comparability. How can the assessment of different elements of the library be weighed against each other? How can the assessment of user education programmes be balanced against the turnaround time for interlibrary loans, for example?

PERFORMANCE ASSESSMENT IN THE PUBLIC SECTOR

This section demonstrates the extent to which the public service sector, including further and higher education and its supporting services, has been influenced by the theory and practice of private sector management. Indeed, performance assessment itself has its roots in the private sector, although over the last fifteen years it has been both adopted and adapted by many public institutions, particularly in the fields of health care (Jenkins *et al.* 1988), education (Cave *et al.* 1988), and local (Rogers, 1990) and central government (Lewis, 1986). Performance assessment criteria, specifically in the form of performance indicators, have been taken up by the proponents of the 'new managerialism', chiefly in order to satisfy the need for accountability, both managerial and political (Jackson, 1993).

A number of management functions which have had their spiritual home in the private sector have now become standard features of many further and higher education establishments. This convergence between managing private and public sector organizations has resulted in many private sector management techniques being utilized or emphasized in the public services sector including customer orientation, strategic planning, aggressive marketing, income generation etc. (Flynn 1993).

The language and practices of 'business' are also becoming

common within this sector. It is the subordination of the public
sector to politics rather than to the market which represents the
main distinction between the two sectors. In private sector management the watchwords are efficiency, rationality and profit
maximization; in the public sector compromise, consensus and
democratic participation.

The 'new managerialism'

Although the current thinking in managerialism is covered in some
depth in Chapter 3, it is worthwhile at this introductory stage to
examine the context in which performance assessment is interwo-
ven into the fabric of management through three major managerial
functions: strategic planning, customer service, and devolving
budgets and responsibilities

Strategic planning

One example of the new managerialism is the introduction of mission
statements, corporate objectives, institutional targets/aims/goals etc.
Whilst the nomenclature is manifold, the subtle nuances which dif-
ferentiate these terms are sometimes lost in the documentation. Most
further and higher education institutions will have mission statements, and most will have produced corporate/business plans which
provide measurable targets. Many of the libraries which support the
courses and programmes delivered at these institutions will also have
identified their own mission statement and strategic plans. Such
commitments should be consistent with and feed into the institutional plans if they are to be meaningful. The degree to which some
institutional commitment to library performance assessment is
included in such statements is explored in Chapter 4. Below are three
examples of mission statements, one taken from a university and two
taken from university library services:

To promote educational opportunity and equality and the application of
knowledge as the means whereby individuals and society may shape and
secure a better future.

Our purpose is to meet the information and media needs of the University
community through the efficiency of our service, the quality of our information resources, the expertise with which we exploit our knowledge,
materials and technology, and the professionalism with which we conduct
our business in the wider world.

The Library's strategy is to work in partnership with academic staff and students to develop effective support for learning. It strives to play an active part in the evolution of the University's educational methods, particularly as regards the planned institutional shift from teaching to learning. Library services will develop in direct response to changes in the information and learning needs of the library's clients – academic staff and students.

The more specific and detailed strategic plans which accompany the mission statements at least provide the institutional and departmental managers (including the librarians) with a baseline from which to assess subsequent performance. The university and college strategic plans, however, remain under political control. For example, the government controls the numbers of students going into post-compulsory education and therefore the resources which accompany them; the capital investments in buildings and infrastructure are also largely government controlled. This political control will win out in the end even though a 'quasi-competitive' market place has been encouraged in terms of:

- the blurring of the binary divide between universities and polytechnics;
- incorporation of further and higher education institutions;
- bidding for resources via research assessment exercises;
- bidding for Follett funds (Joint Funding Councils' Libraries Review Group, 1993);
- production of league tables of institutions including their library services;
- 'encouraging' science/technology students by reducing the amount universities receive for arts students.

Customer service

One of the key management concepts which has successfully made the transfer into the public domain is the emphasis on service to customers (Cook, 1992; St.Clair, 1993; Fielden, 1993). This emphasis placed on the consumer, user, end-user, client, recipient of the service (or however defined) has taken firm root and is manifest in a proliferation of customer care policy statements (see example below), surveys to identify needs, training courses, after-service evaluation, help desks etc. These are explored further in the next chapter. The following is an example of a customer care policy statement:

- We will base present and future services on the needs of our customers.
- We will plan our services realistically and deploy resources where most needed.
- We endeavour at all times to be approachable, to be courteous and helpful, and to treat our customers with respect.
- We aim to run our services in an efficient, effective and professional manner.
- We will ensure that each of our customers is entitled to spend time with appropriate library staff concerning his or her information or service needs.
- We will listen to the comments of our customers.
- We aim to ensure high quality customer service by encouraging and providing appropriate development and training of all library staff.
- We will endeavour to keep customers and colleagues informed of library activities, policies and developments.

This ethos has permeated much of the public service sector so that services aim to meet the needs of the customer rather than the organization. For many organizations this has involved a cultural shift, with attendant changes in attitudes, values and assumptions. Quality of service has become an overriding concern.

The promotion by Peters and Waterman (1982) of the 'close to the consumer' philosophy represented one of the early driving forces of this concept borrowed from the US business world. The Local Government Training Board (1987) is a prime example of the practical ways in which this customer-oriented ethos has developed in the local government arena. This attitude has also reached into other public sector services particularly the Civil Service, the National Health Service as well as the police and education services. The advent of charterism considered in Chapter 2 represents an almost natural follow-on.

Pollitt (1988) amongst others recognized that the recipients of a particular service should be involved not only in its planning and organization but also in its monitoring and evaluation. Performance assessment therefore needs to take into account the views of the recipients. This perspective is discussed in Chapter 2 and revisited in the final chapter.

Devolving budgets and responsibilities

Since 1979 there has been a continuous drive to emulate the private sector in devolving financial and other managerial responsibilities. The economistic nature of the new managerialism is reflected in this desire to ensure that public expenditure goes as far as possible to produce efficiency and value for money. The devolution has occurred on a macro scale in the Civil Service ('Next Steps' agencies), the Health Service (Hospital Trusts and general practitioner fundholding) and education (local management of schools and corporate status for polytechnics). The policy has also been pursued on a micro scale within institutions, for example the devolution of budgets to cost centres – faculties, library, computer services – in further and higher education and sometimes even further down to sub(ject) librarians with financial and other responsibilities. For the first time many middle/lower level staff are exercising the responsibilities of identifying costs, monitoring spending and accounting for financial performance of their units/sections/departments. Alongside these must lie performance assessment measures, be they related to finance, for example efficiency measures, or to staffing, for example performance appraisal (the latter is considered in Chapter 8). These tasks are currently made more difficult by the Government's policy of financing any expansion of higher education through additional productivity gains as the unit of resource is inevitably lowered.

The influence of business techniques in the further and higher education sectors has necessitated a greater emphasis on income generation, efficiency savings, marketing exercises in a quasi-competitive environment and also the search for alternative forms of course or programme delivery to ever increasing numbers of students, for example access, franchise, distance/open learning etc. Post-school education is seen nowadays as a consumption or investment good rather than a citizen right. Consequently academic libraries have been obliged to be a part of this process and performance assessment has become one tool with which to evaluate progress so that policies for improvement may be implemented.

FURTHER READING

Abbott, C. (1994) *Performance Measurement in Library and Information Services*. London: Aslib.

Blagden, J. and Harrington, J. (1990) *How Good is Your Library? A*

Review of Approaches to the Evaluation of Library and Information Services. London: Aslib.

British Journal of Academic Librarianship (1989) **4**(2) is a special issue devoted to performance assessment including papers by Brophy, Ford and Lines.

Flynn, N. (1993) *Public Sector Management* (2nd ed.). Hemel Hempstead: Harvester Wheatsheaf.

Goodall, D. L. (1988) 'Performance measurement: a historical perspective'. *Journal of Librarianship* **20**(2), 128–144.

Kantor, P. (1984) *Objective Performance Measures for Academic and Research Libraries*. Washington: Association of Research Libraries.

Lancaster, F. W. (1993) *If You Want to Evaluate Your Library ...* (2nd rev ed.). London: Library Association Publishing.

McDonald, J. A. and Micikas, L. B. (1994) *Academic Libraries: the Dimensions of Their Effectiveness*. Westport, Ct.: Greenwood Press.

Van House, N., Weil, B. T. and McClure, C. R. (1990) *Measuring Academic Library Performance: a Practical Approach*. Chicago: American Library Association.

Winkworth, I. (1990) 'Performance indicators for polytechnic libraries.' *Library Review* **39**(5), 23–41.

CHAPTER TWO

The consumer perspective

If you are providing a service there will always be a subjective element
in assessing quality; and ... the most important judge is the customer.
(Booth, 1993, p.7)

what libraries should mostly be concerned with measuring is
their ultimate product – performance or effectiveness – and the
best indicators of their level of performance are, or should be,
based on user data such as satisfaction.
(Powell, 1988, p.34)

For all practical purposes user satisfaction must be disregarded
as anything other than a supportive measure.
(McMurdo, 1980, p.83)

Blagden (1988) maintains that performance assessment should be
based on what users actually do rather than what they say they do.
(Blagden and Harrington, 1990, p.13)

The issues covered in this chapter are:

- the importance of the users to library service assessment;
- users' expectations;
- the customer-orientation approach.

In considering the users of the library service, complexity dictates
that the issues are categorized into convenient sections. However, in
so doing, it is not the intention to underestimate the interconnectivity
between the various elements which make up the library–user interface but only to attempt some clarity of thought. Figure 2.1 shows the
complexity of the relationships between these elements and below
are some examples within each of the categories.

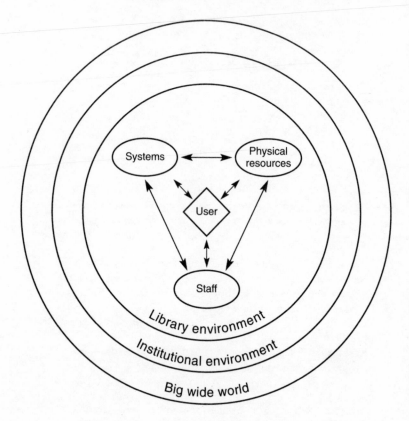

Figure 2.1. Library-user environment

Systems
Book and periodical classification schemes, indexing and abstracting systems, physical layout of the library, parallel sequences, issue and return protocols, overdue and fines regimes, manual and electronic catalogues, enquiry services, general rules and regulations, security systems etc.

Physical resources
Books, periodicals, audio-visual material, electronic databases and allied services, seating and different types of furniture, photocopying and other reprographic equipment etc.

Staff
The different roles of library staff – which to approach in terms of subject knowledge, function, competences, levels within the library hierarchy. What are the users expectations of the staff and are these realistic?

Library environment
Silent study areas, group study areas, bookable carrels; quiet/noisy atmosphere; heating, lighting, general comfort; accessibility of the library, its services and the material for able or disabled users; the library's size and the implications for user apprehension/intimidation etc.

Institutional environment
How supportive of the library is the institutional management both politically and economically? How close is the relationship between departments and the library, between other support services and the library particularly computing services.

Big wide world
How influential is the government of the day in terms of resources and rhetoric? What are the effects of government policies on the library service in terms of capital expenditure, development etc? How dependent are the institutions on technological advances in computing, networking, telecommunications etc?

Users
What personal 'baggage' do users bring to the library – the image of libraries and librarians promoted by the mass media, users' previous experiences of other libraries, their previous education and/or employment experience, their levels of information handling and literacy, willingness to take responsibility for their own learning. Users have their own personal constraints in terms of time, finance, social activities etc.

It should be acknowledged at this early stage that the nomenclature surrounding the library user is, to say the least, varied and for the purposes of this chapter, largely synonymous. Although the preference of the author is for the term 'user', throughout the text other terms are adopted; these include 'reader', 'client', 'customer', 'consumer', 'student' (the term 'patron' is used mainly in the US).

THE IMPORTANCE OF THE USER

The inclusion of the quotations at the head of this chapter demonstrates the diversity of views on the library users' opinions and
attitudes towards the service. The views of these commentators
represent differences of emphasis. Generally, there is little disagreement about the importance of the user in the service
assessment process. However, whether that assessment should
involve the collection of data in the form of users' views and attitudes remains a matter for debate. The change of emphasis lies in
the perceived significance of such views within the overall assessment process. On the one hand user satisfaction levels could form a
central plank of a library's performance assessment policy with
other more objective measures as supporting evidence. This seems
to be the tenor of the quotations from both Booth and Powell. The
implication of the quotations both from McMurdo and from
Blagden and Harrington is that users' views should act as supporting data if they are to be used at all. The overriding view arising
out of the literature is that any performance assessment policy or
programme which excludes the opinions of the users provides an
incomplete picture. The extent to which such views are taken into
account will depend on the nature of the activity under scrutiny
and will be a matter for professional judgement. For example, it
would be difficult to conceive of the evaluation of a readers'
enquiry service without some recognition of the quality, accuracy
and competence of the service from the enquirer's point of view.

Involvement of the service users in judging the success of that
service makes sense for a number of reasons and is reflected in the
SCONUL approach (Chapter 10). A sentence one sometimes hears
in academic libraries goes something like this: 'If the students
weren't around, our jobs wouldn't be necessary'. Whilst stating the
glaringly obvious, it does highlight the main reason for the
library's existence and provides a sometimes necessary jolt to
remind some library staff of this. By becoming 'bogged down' in
layers of backroom processes and activities, whether it is book
processing, entering periodical subscriptions or staff appraisal
interviews, it is easy to forget the library's *raison d'être*. The attitude of some library staff is more along the lines of:'If the students
weren't around, we could get on with our work!'. Within the last
two decades there has been a gradual move in the academic sector,
and perhaps in the wider profession, from concentrating on looking

inwards to a more outward approach. Examples of the former would include the efficiency of internal processes, integrating computing and housekeeping facilities and (some would say) an over emphasis on classification and cataloguing principles. The more outward approach emphasizes the needs of the user, service orientation and the nowadays ubiquitous customer care philosophy (Line, 1991). This is taken up later in the chapter.

Inevitably, one of the aims of academic libraries, however differently worded, will be to satisfy the information needs of the user population. According to some, the best way to gauge satisfaction levels is to ask the users, which brings us back to the quotations at the head of the chapter. Indeed, the Local Government Training Board (1987, p.5) is quite categorical in its view that 'satisfactory service cannot be provided unless the views of customers are taken into account'. Unfortunately, a certain intellectual and methodological snobbery has developed around the adoption of subjective measures in contributing to the performance assessment picture. As Pollitt (1986, p.82) remarks quite rightly 'there is actually nothing inherently inferior in measures of "feelings" or perceptions or judgements'. The most important question is what is done with these subjective comments to help arrive at an assessment outcome.

One fundamental reason for the inclusion of users' views whenever possible is to counterbalance the views of some academic librarians who purport to 'know' – as if by instinct or intuition – the users' views. This is sometimes referred to as professional judgement built on years of experience. Such putative knowledge may indeed have accurate foundations but may also be based on misconceptions, distortion, biases, or anecdotal or unrepresentative evidence. Any of these may be acting as substitutes for knowledge of users' views. The whole issue of academic library surveys is covered in Chapter 9.

Ensuring that the views which are communicated to the library staff are representative of particular groups rather than personal wants, needs, demands or whinges can be problematic. The opinions garnered from course monitoring and evaluation procedures may be interesting, informative and helpful to the library, but a cautious approach is advised because of possible misrepresentation. Similarly, subject or liaison librarians will often attend course meetings, focus/discussion groups or library committees where library problems affecting courses are discussed. Although it is intended that students should be representing their colleagues and expressing the collective view, there is sometimes the danger of personal problems being peddled. This difficulty is exemplified in Blagden and Harrington (1990, p.13) quoting Brember and Leggate (1985):

Very active users (who account for a high proportion of all use) can dis-
tort the perceptions of library staff about the whole user community and
thus obscure the needs of both the less active and the non-user.

Connected with understanding the users' needs is the idea of view-ing the library service *from their perspective*. As indicated above, librarians have developed values, attitudes and cultural norms which play a part in their approach to work and in their adoption and use of systems and processes to meet the information needs of the academic community. It may be necessary sometimes to challenge those taken-for-granted ideas so that librarians are able, whenever possi-ble, to see through the eyes of the user. A similar problem, although arising in a different but related context – education, may provide a helpful insight into observing/viewing users. When carrying out research studies in school classrooms, Delamont (1981) highlighted the difficulty of seeing in a different light the normal, the usual, the ordinary, the commonplace, the routine, the everyday. To gain poss-ibly novel insights into the teaching and learning activities and relationships amongst the participants it is necessary 'to make the familiar strange' (p.71) – indeed, to challenge the taken-for-granted. The following are three suggestions that could be incorporated into the academic library context:

- To study, observe or participate in non-library settings which are chosen for their parallel features, for example attendance at lectures or seminars (either sitting in or observing) or observ-ing other service providers (health-related professions such as doctors and dentists, retail outlets, civil service outlets, Citizens' Advice Bureaux, tourist offices etc.). This forces the librarian to regard services and their quality from the viewpoint of the recipient.
- To make use of other academic libraries and carry out some of the procedures that students themselves carry out in one's own library. Examples could include accessibility and availability of the books, periodicals and other services, use of the cata-logues, effectiveness of guiding and signposting.

- To encourage someone who is unfamiliar with the library to do as in the above suggestion and discuss later the ease or difficulty of using the facilities and services.

Without wishing to overstate the case, these activities are intended to illustrate the potential for avoiding the perpetuation of misguided views.

A final reason for involving users in the assessment process is the expectation that they *should* be involved. A variety of movements including charterism (and student charters in particular) and consumer rights, together with the greater emphasis on accountability and value for money have been, and continue to be, well documented in the mass media and have formed an important part of the government's public sector policy. This area was alluded to in the previous chapter.

USERS' EXPECTATIONS

When discussing the expectations of library service users it is worth reflecting on the heterogeneous nature of the people who constitute the potential user population. Undoubtedly, one of the aspirations of the library is to satisfy the information needs of this divergent group within the available resources. To demonstrate this heterogeneity, the following represent some of the categories into which users may be divided: full-time and part-time students; those on short courses or sandwich, day release, access, franchise, compact, distance or open learning courses; academic, research, administrative, clerical, technical staff and teaching assistants; students attending evening classes and those studying for GCSE/Advanced Level, as well as undergraduate, postgraduate and research students; corporate users and those employed in local businesses and professions; Open University students and those studying at other institutions; foreign students, mature students, those from ethnic minorities or with disabilities; ex-employees or ex-students; the general public. The list could go on and on.

The point to make is that the needs and particularly the expectations of individuals (and they are individual bodies and minds not FTEs!) within these groups will form a wide spectrum. Library managers must perform a delicate balancing act to find out different needs, to ensure expectations remain realistic whenever possible, to provide an appropriate range of services and to assess their effectiveness.

Much speculation has revolved around the 'goodness' of a library and the problems of defining such a quality. Orr (1973), Buckland (1982) and Line (1990) have all pondered the notion without necessarily coming to any consensus. Similarly, many library users – and indeed non-users – will have their own views on what constitutes a good library and these views may act as a benchmark when making judgements in the future. Conversely, many students progressing from school to further or higher education may never have set foot in a library or at least have only had experience of the school library. Their expectations of what will greet them on arrival in the groves of academe will depend upon a number of past cultural encounters including the image of libraries and librarians portrayed in the media. There was an example in a recent television 'soap' in which one character said: 'a librarian and interesting; isn't that a contradiction in terms?'. Expectations of students who have studied at a further education establishment and made use of its library/resources centre or who have made regular visits to public libraries may be suitably raised when being thrust into the university library environment.

It is also true to say that expectations will alter over the duration of a course or programme of study. This change may depend on a number of variables: the user's initial competence and application of previously and newly acquired skills to the library's systems; the self-confidence and self-reliance that should come with learning and practice; or the early interactions with library staff that may influence a user's attitude to the whole service either temporarily or permanently. For these reasons the early stages of library induction and orientation can be critical in ensuring that the student's expectations of service provision remain realistic. At times librarians are at fault by raising expectations, albeit for altruistic reasons. They want desperately to please the user and provide him/her with an efficient and effective service. It is therefore important that the library staff aim to under-promise and over-deliver rather than vice versa.

A complex array of personal 'baggage' including past experience(s) and other psychological phenomena, for example confidence, assertiveness, motivation, will accompany these students. Some will view the scene positively and optimistically as an opportunity to make the library work for them. For others the expectation may be that this huge intimidating resource will present a series of hoops through which they are expected to jump.

Such hoops could be physical, organizational, linguistic or attitudinal. It is at this fairly early stage that some students may withdraw from the challenge. Their expectations may be such that they feel unable to cope with the requirements placed upon them, and consequently their use of the library service remains at the most basic level. One would like to think that these students represent only a small minority, but who knows? Even from students in the latter stages of a course it is an all too frequent cry of desperation that can be heard 'I haven't got a clue where to start'.

Emphasis should also be placed on the dual commitment which is implicit in most library performance assessment – the expectation that users will make the most of the available library and information skills training (both formal and informal) to get the best out of the service. The two sides need to meet somewhere in the middle.

CUSTOMER-ORIENTATION APPROACH

[University library services] have to be more responsive to students who are seen increasingly – and see themselves – as customers.

(Feather and Marriott, 1993, p.29)

As indicated in the above quotation and the previous chapter this concentration on the customer – almost obsessional in some quarters – has had considerable influence not only in the commercial sector but also in many public sector services. This orientation has shown itself under many guises, some of which will be explored here and are included in the library consumerism model in Figure 2.2. This model places the signs of customer orientation on a spectrum ranging from the more shallow variety to the provision of the virtual library with self-service, open access etc. One might say in admittedly rather crude terms that it moves from cosmetics to consumerism. A recent example of the right-hand end of the spectrum is the student-driven approach at Thames Valley University (Dolphin, 1994). This learning resource centre has been created with the explicit intention of responding directly to students' wishes and streamlining procedures through 'process modelling'. Some commentators (St.Clair, 1993) view the so-called cosmetic elements as a legitimate means of being seen to provide an effective professional service, and this may indeed be the case. Although considered in another service context LeBoeuf (1989)

Figure 2.2. One library 'consumer' model.

terms this the 'showbiz' approach. These customer care initiatives may or may not be successful in the long term but will certainly work at 'the moment of truth' defined as 'any episode in which the customer comes into contact with any aspect of the organisation and gets an impression of the quality of the service'(Albrecht, 1992, p.26). Through the model various devices for exchanges of information are used. These are followed by the application of such information to a greater commitment to the customer.

Focusing on library users and their needs can lead to a mismatch in philosophies. To illustrate this one need look no further than the gradual shift from a teacher- to a learner-centred approach to education which has taken over in further and higher education particularly in the last decade. Whilst many educationists have moved in the direction of this pedagogical change, they have not necessarily convinced those in the student body to fall in line behind. These two scenarios provide a flavour of the friction which may result.

Scenario 1

One of the aims of a university library is to provide the users with the appropriate skills to become independent and self-reliant in their use of libraries and information. Some cynics have termed this the BOFOFY method – buzz off and find out for yourself! However, some users will either be unaware of or will disagree with this aim, or indeed the urgency of the information requirement may be such that the route to that information is of little interest. What the users may want is the specific information need satisfied and they want it as near to now as possible! Perhaps some students' interpretation of the student-centred approach implies aiming to satisfy needs immediately.

Scenario 2

It is one element of the collection development policy of a university library that multiple copies of book titles are discouraged in favour of single/double copies of a wider range of titles, that is, pursuing breadth in favour of depth. Whilst the arguments in favour of this policy are well rehearsed on educational and economic grounds, the policy seems to flounder on customer-orientation grounds. Is it so unreasonable that year on year the major comment on course monitoring and evaluation seems to be 'insufficient copies of texts'?

These are examples of situations in which the customers may agree, with some justification, that the orientation towards them is less than credible. The process of changing people's expectations can be a very slow one.

CHARTERISM

In tandem with a heightened concern for the end-user of a service has been the arrival of charterism emanating from the government's support of the Citizen's Charter (Her Majesty's Stationery Office, 1991). The principles that are reflected in the charter movement are standards, information and openness, choice and consultation, courtesy and helpfulness, putting things right and value for money. Only the most cynical would argue against these as principles to which public service organizations should aspire. Indeed many will argue that they successfully put these into practice daily. There are currently forty published Government charters including a Department for Education Charter for Higher Education. The movement has also spawned a plethora of other charters such as a National Union of Students (NUS) Charter, and some universities have published their own, for example Sheffield Hallam and South Bank. Such library charters set out the rights of the users and the kind and (in some cases) standards of service they are entitled to receive. Examples are: a commitment to responding to 75% of enquiries immediately and dealing with specialist enquiries requiring referrals within three working days; obtaining available material from other campus libraries within five working days.

Conversely, the responsibilities of the users may also be set out in the same document, thus recognizing a reciprocal commitment. Examples are: treating all library materials with respect; purchasing core texts as recommended by tutors.

The charter movement has succeeded in highlighting the fact that consumers have rights in the public services as in other sectors. This move has contributed, albeit in a minor way, to the greater assertiveness of users within the academic community. Unless it is regarded as one of the latest fashions, charterism may also have the knock-on effects of improving communication with library users, demonstrating a commitment to quality, and focusing the attention of library staff on specific service issues.

NON-USERS

Many surveys only consider library users – we need access to non-users also and investigate information sources THEY use; presumably they get their information from somewhere.

(FE College Librarian from survey in Chapter 4)

It may be worthwhile spending a few moments reflecting on those who make little or no use of the library, and their reasons for it. There are few substantial empirical studies of this phenomenon within the academic library sector; this is partly due to the nature of its captive audience. Instances have been recorded where students have made no use of their own university library but this has not hindered their ability to gain the required qualifications. Indeed, one member of the academic staff of the author's university registered with the library on his arrival in post in 1990 and had yet to borrow a book before leaving in late 1994. In such cases, how are information and research needs being satisfied? One would expect that the academic staff would require library services of a high order to support their research and consultancy work. Perhaps the extent of their social and academic networking – via telephone, electronic and conventional mail, bulletin boards, professional and academic literature and conferences, as well as personal and departmental collections – is greater than is generally appreciated. Certainly the advent of CAS-IAS services (Current Alerting Services combined with Individual Article Supply) such as UnCover and the British Library's Inside Information are bringing the researcher and the document together and in so doing potentially bypassing the library completely (Woodward, 1994). Line's INFROSS studies (1971) and the more recent work of Slater (1989) indicate that librarians play a largely peripheral part in the life of the (applied) social science researcher. There is no reason to think that the situation has improved for the library, given the information technology developments and the traditionally more close-knit community of science academics.

Possibly some students may purchase all the necessary items and avoid the journal literature altogether. Possibly some students receive all the information they need through networking and sharing, together with lecture notes, handouts etc. Others may make use of public libraries or other academic libraries which are more conveniently located. Much more work needs to be done on the extent of and reasons for non-use.

FURTHER READING

Bawden, D. (1990) *User-Oriented Evaluation of Information Systems and Services*. Aldershot: Gower.

Cook, S. (1992) *Customer Care: Implementing Total Quality in Today's Service-Driven Organisation*. London: Kogan Page.

Local Government Training Board (1987) *Getting Closer to the Public*. Luton: Local Government Training Board.

Lund, K. and Patterson, H. (1994) *Customer Care*. London: Association of Assistant Librarians (Group of the Library Association).

Pollitt, C. (1988) 'Bringing consumers into performance measurement: concepts, consequences and constraints.' *Policy and Politics* **16** (2), 77–87.

St.Clair, G. (1993) *Customer Service in the Information Environment*. London: Bowker Saur.

Smith, I. (1994) *Meeting Customer Needs*. Oxford: Butterworth-Heinemann.

Whittaker, K. (1993) *Basics of Library-Based User Services*. London: Library Association Publishing.

CHAPTER THREE

A managerial perspective

MIKE HEERY

> I want you to tell me what's wrong with me and MGM – even if
> it means losing your job.
>
> Sam Goldwyn

The issues covered in this chapter include:

- performance assessment in the context of the managerialist model;
- the importance of participation and strategic planning;
- the problems of day to day management of library service performance.

Sam Goldwyn's characteristic comment conveys quite well the sense of threat that is often associated with performance assessment. Whether the assessment takes the form of the appraisal of individuals (Chapter 8) or the assessment of services (Chapters 5–7), it has the potential to unsettle public sector professionals. It has connotations of control that could be harsh and impersonal, or unsympathetic to the subtleties of professional practices. These anxieties are sharply focused when the issue of performance-related pay is raised. What could be more threatening than having the security of salary undermined by performance assessment? Such fears have been apparent in UK higher education in recent years, as they have in other areas of the public sector. For example, the introduction of new contracts for polytechnic lecturers in 1992 was bedevilled by suspicion about the government's motives in introducing performance appraisal. Also higher education has had the experience of other professional groups to consider. For example, performance bonuses were first introduced into the Civil Service in 1987, and by 1993 25% of UK local authorities had performance-related pay schemes (Local Government Management Board, 1994).

The purpose of this chapter is to consider performance assessment from the perspective of those managing academic libraries. Are performance indicators threatening, or are they a useful addition to the toolkit of management techniques? What effect will performance assessment have within the library? Can it influence the position of the library within the larger institution? In seeking to answer such questions this chapter tries to consider the issues in such a way as to be of use to practising librarians. It is, therefore, appropriate to place performance assessment firmly within the context of what academic librarians are trying to achieve more widely. All libraries are under pressure as a result of the continual need to secure resources during a time of considerable change. Those managing academic libraries have a large number of issues to contend with. Where does performance assessment fit in?

THE RISE OF MANAGERIALISM

It is important to review how academic librarians come to find themselves grappling with management techniques such as performance indicators. It can be safely assumed that most of those now in senior positions in UK academic libraries have had little formal education in management. They are unlikely to have entered librarianship because of an interest in management. Yet the environment in which they now work is increasingly concerned with management concepts and their practical application. Librarians need to be able to relate issues such as performance assessment to wider ideas about how organizations should be managed.

It is notable how quickly the terminology of performance assessment has been absorbed into UK further and higher education in recent years. Here is the opening paragraph of the chapter on library management from the Follett report:

Given the importance of information provision in higher education institutions, its effective management is essential. This chapter discusses the place of the library and of its staff in the work of the institutions whose activities they support, and how it needs to be addressed. It also covers three areas where the Review Group considers that specific action will bring valuable benefits. These are: strategic planning, and the context in which this needs to take place; the development and use of performance indicators; and staff management. (Joint Funding Councils' Libraries Review Group, 1993, p.27)

Some academic librarians may be surprised at the report's emphasis on management. However, in the 1990s this emphasis on management is not at all unusual. It is part of a significant change in how public sector organizations are run, and one which affects further and higher education as much as any other service.

This change can be understood as a move from the concept of professional public administration to that of public management. The rise of managerialism, or the new public management as it is sometimes called, is mentioned in the opening chapter of this book. It is worth considering concepts such as managerialism so as to try to decide whether academic librarians should adopt new forms of management in a spirit of positive agreement, or whether they should remain suspicious of them.

There is no shortage of controversy about the introduction of management practices into the UK public sector. The term 'managerialism' is often used pejoratively, for it has many critics. It describes the organizational and managerial changes which have taken place in public services in recent years. It comprises a number of key aspects of management. These include: the use of strategic planning to set clear objectives; setting managers targets of performance; developing performance indicators to aid the measurement of organizational achievement; changing the culture of public services from public service values to market-led, entrepreneurial values; introducing individual appraisal for all employees; and developing a service orientation responsive to the needs of clients or customers.

In addition, 'managerialism also encompasses a set of ideas and values justifying a central role for managers and management within organisations and society' (Farnham and Horton, 1993, p.238). As such it challenges traditional notions of public administration, as well as the practices of professional groups. Above all, managerialism is an agent for change within organizations. It rejects traditional values, replacing them with strategies that evolve in response to changing environmental factors, such as resource levels. According to Pollitt (1993, p.5) the new public management is 'the search for the best use of resources in pursuit of objectives subject to change'. It is not therefore inherently sympathetic to notions of the public good, such as the value of education for its own sake.

The widespread distrust of managerialism amongst public service professionals lies in its close association with the right wing governments of Reagan, Thatcher and Major. There is no doubt that these governments have used the concepts of business management to weaken both professionals (such as doctors and teachers) and trade unionists. Under these regimes the new public management has become associated with a high degree of control. Governments have used management techniques to secure the reduction of public sector costs. The mechanisms of managerialism have been used to implement government objectives. In this respect the processes of management may well have been used selectively. For example, it has been argued that under Thatcher 'the emphasis is more on control, and less on planning; more on finance and less on establishing formal organisational structures' (Pollitt, 1993, p.4).

Performance assessment clearly fits into this notion of controlling public organizations to ensure that they meet objectives. Education, the NHS, central and local government have all been affected. It has been observed that 'it is in the former polytechnics and institutions of higher education that the managerialist thrust in higher education has become most institutionalised' (Farnham and Horton, 1993, p.246).

Universities have also adopted managerialism. The Jarratt Report (1985) argues that 'a range of performance indicators should be developed, covering both inputs and outputs and designed for use both within individual institutions and for making comparisons between institutions' (Johnes and Taylor, 1990, p.4). The new managerialism clearly affects everyone working in further and higher education, including librarians. At the same time it is natural to be aware of the suspicion surrounding techniques such as performance measurement. Henty (1989, p.77), for example, attributes the appearance of performance assessment in academic libraries to the desire of governments to make financial savings:

The evaluation of programs in the public sector has become more necessary in recent years as governments have sought to cut back on expenditure. The theory that institutions have definable outcomes which can be readily measured has gained increasing credibility, and has put pressure on institutions in the educational and cultural spheres to state their objectives and develop techniques to measure them. In the library context, this has led to a situation in which library services are being seen in terms of measurable activity rather than as a generalised public good.

Should librarians connive at the introduction of measures that may originate in objectives concerned with cost-cutting and control? Should librarians adopt the management ideas of those who seem unsympathetic to what we in publicly funded post-compulsory education are trying to achieve?

In the view of the author it is necessary to provide a view of management that appreciates what is useful in the new managerialism but which rejects the severe control that is implicit in Thatcherism. In other words, librarians need a positive view of management before they can tackle the question of performance assessment. The measurement of performance only makes sense as a component in a general managerial approach.

PARTICIPATIVE MANAGERIALISM

I believe that librarians can adopt a managerial approach that is in harmony with the cultural or educational ethos of the university or college. Management skills are not incompatible with public sector or academic values. The severely controlling elements of the new managerialism can be jettisoned, whilst much that is of use may be retained. There is a great deal of value to the librarian in a modern managerial approach. The skills that comprise management can both improve the internal life of the library and also strengthen its institutional position. To do so, however, the management approach must not be mechanistic or based upon rigid systems. It must be closely attuned to the environment around it. The manager must be in harmony with the academic culture of the university, as well as the life of the library. The academic library manager needs an understanding of education and of librarianship first of all. Management skills are tools that can be made to work for the positive educational or professional goals of the library. Line (1990, p.261) has argued that '"management" should be seen not as antipathetic to scholarship and professional knowledge, but as using them on behalf of the service'. The skills associated with strategic planning, resource allocation and performance assessment are not of themselves politically biased. They are essentially an effective means of getting things done. They are a means of addressing the growing number of issues that seem to face academic libraries.

Managerialism offers a set of tools to those running libraries that are not only useful but also timely. They are the appropriate tools for dealing with the issues of the 1990s. In one sense this is true simply because the concepts of managerialism are becoming the common currency of everyone's working life. Most large organizations of whatever sort are managed via strategic planning, the setting of goals and objectives, performance measurement and review. In other words, librarians cannot afford to stand back from the managerial concepts by which work and organizations are increasingly interpreted.

There are, however, two more fundamental reasons why the adoption of a managerial approach is important. The first has been articulated by Noon (1991, p.9) in a persuasive article which explains why management skills are now essential for librarians. The crux of his argument is that

markets, information and budgets do not have independent lives of their own; they all rely on the abilities and skills of the people who have the responsibility for them. The effective manager is the one who is able to get the best results out of the staff in these areas in pursuit of their common goal. In other words, if you want it summarised in one of those glib one-liners of which management teaching is so fond: *management is achieving results through people*.

Academic libraries are often large, employing many people. Those people need to achieve results to enable the library to solve its problems and to enact new developments. The days of authoritarian dictat are over (at least in most libraries!). To be effective librarians need to organize – or manage – their staff effectively. This is unlikely to happen unless management skills are employed. Careful nurturing of sound staff development policies and of genuinely participative management will motivate staff, improve job satisfaction and lead to better decision-making in pursuit of goals that are understood and shared by everyone. This people-oriented management approach is a beneficial outcome of the new managerialism. Specific techniques such as performance assessment must be considered in terms of their effect upon the overall participative method of management. Performance indicators that are not supported by the staff because they are too mechanistic or too impersonal will not be of any use. Similarly, individual appraisal should be a positive development, motivating staff and providing a healthy stimulus to their work. It can of course be handled very differently, with serious consequences, as Chapter 8 outlines. A people-oriented approach to management is also in tune with a general societal change, whereby individuals are less deferential and more ready to participate, to make suggestions, and to understand the context within which they work. The weakening of hierarchical staff structures is, therefore, both timely and beneficial.

The second important reason why management skills are important is that they equip organizations to deal with change. Academic libraries are increasingly having to change. This is largely as a result of changes at institutional level. Further and higher education in the UK has altered profoundly in recent years. The rationalization of a multi-site university has meant libraries having to merge. The absorption of a college into a university or the amalgamation of tertiary and further education colleges have profoundly changed respective library services. Libraries have been brought together with media units, reprographics facilities or, increasingly, computer centres.

Other educational changes are affecting libraries. The growth in student numbers is an obvious example. Others are the modularization of courses, the increase in distance learning courses, the rise in the numbers of part-time students and the growth of access/franchise arrangements. The resourcing of libraries has been subject to considerable change. A further set of changes result from technological advances. The way in which educational institutions operate is being changed by the growth of computer networking, with obvious implications for libraries. Indeed, the rate of technological change means that libraries must alter their staff structures if employees are to keep their own development in tune with what is happening. Decision-making will have to speed up in the new IT environment. As staffing levels are unlikely to expand to any great extent, more staff will have to be included in the process of making decisions. It is likely that staff structures will have to become flatter.

STRATEGIC MANAGERIALISM

Management skills, such as strategic planning, are essential for the librarian faced with change. If change is not to be experienced as something that just happens to the library, with unknown consequences, the library must actively deal with new situations. Strategic planning is a tool for tackling change head on, so as to control it. In fact many of the changes taking place in further and higher education offer opportunities to libraries. These opportunities are more likely to be taken where the library employs carefully planned strategies with clear objectives.

In answer to the question 'Why plan?' Corrall (1994, p.3) states that:

planning helps us to prepare for a better future ... strategic planning fulfils
the dual role of relating an organisation and its people to the environment
and providing unity and direction to its activities.

The techniques of strategic planning help the manager to analyse the
changing environment. For example, the librarian needs a clear
analysis of both the current situation and how the institution is
going to change over the next few years. What are our strengths and
weaknesses? How will the forthcoming changes affect the library,
and what should be done as a result? These questions can be
answered by using strategic planning. This is because strategic planning is not an intellectual activity that is separate from day to day
work. In a properly managed library strategic planning is an integral
part of the day to day work. It facilitates the organizational responsiveness that is needed in a period of change. Corrall (1994, p.4)
maintains that:

Strategic planning is a process in which purposes, objectives and plans are
formulated, and then implemented; both formulation and implementation
processes are evolutionary and continuous. It is a process of relating an
organisation to its changing market opportunities, a key concern being the
pressures, constraints, opportunities and threats within the sector in which
it competes or operates.

In terms of academic libraries, the 'organisation' that Corrall refers
to is the library, and the 'sector' is the parent institution.

Strategic planning requires the participation of staff. It is not a
remote process. The senior managers of the library may have greater
input into the analysis of the library's changing environment.
However, staff at all levels should be involved in deciding upon specific goals and how to implement them. This emphasis on the
involvement of staff raises again the importance of the participative
style of management already referred to. Participation will not
happen without careful planning. Where there has been a lack of
participation in the past people will at first be reluctant to contribute, even when they are offered opportunities to do so. Managers
need to set up structures that allow consultation and the exchange of
ideas to occur. For example, at the University of the West of
England library policies are formulated in a Policy Committee of 18
staff members. All groups of staff are represented. The Committee is
a real policy-making body that can reject the proposals of senior
managers, and indeed has done so. The committee is supported by a

series of other meetings, where staff can decide upon policy proposals in the company of their peers. Decisions taken in the Policy
Committee are often implemented via small working groups specifically set up for the task, and which contain staff from different
areas. This kind of structure fits reasonably well with the requirements of strategic planning in a large library, as long as it has the
active support of staff.

Strategic management is not only relevant within the library. The
formulation of a strategic plan is also important in relation to the
wider institution. Many libraries are required to formulate a strategic plan as part of a wider planning process. They agree annual
targets or planning agreements with the institutional executive. In
one sense, therefore, the formulation of a strategic plan can simply
be a part of how things are done across the institution. The planning
process is most useful, however, where it helps to *influence* the
institutional executive. It then provides a means of keeping library
issues before institutional policy-makers and allows the librarian to
show how library strategies relate to institution-wide strategies. It
can help to tie the library closely into general institutional planning.

Performance assessment follows naturally from a commitment to
strategic planning and to a managerial approach. The pursuit of
strategic objectives requires that an assessment is made of whether
they are being met. Performance assessment is the means by which
the library checks that what the library is actually doing is in support of the agreed objectives. As Abbott (1994, p.13) suggests:

The statement of library objectives provides the framework within which
performance indicators should be developed. ... the planning process
involving objective setting, resource allocation and performance evaluation is not linear, but cyclical. Performance indicators are both informed by
and inform the strategic objectives.

Indeed, 'the monitoring process is crucial at all levels; if neglected,
plans cease to function as working tools' (Corrall, 1994, p.41). A
commitment to a managerial approach will, therefore, necessarily
require a commitment to performance assessment.

THE MANAGEMENT OF PERFORMANCE ASSESSMENT

The remainder of this chapter will explore how managers can in
practice develop suitable measures of performance, and it will do so
from two different perspectives. First, it will look at the relevance of

performance assessment to the library's external environment. Then
it will consider the management of evaluation within the libraries.
In both these dimensions there are a range of issues facing the
library manager.

Accountability

The external relevance of performance assessment lies in the
accountability of academic libraries to their institutions, and beyond
them the funding councils. UK funding councils are currently developing a range of audit and assessment measures with the aim of
evaluating the performance of institutions in the further and higher
education sectors (see Chapter 4). Richard's (1992, p.22) research
has concluded that 'the most widely quoted reason for interest in
performance indicators is outside pressure'. This accountability of
libraries is an integral part of the new managerialism in higher education. Libraries are expensive to run and in a period of change are
bound to come under scrutiny.

As institutions have become more accountable to funding bodies, so
departments have become accountable to institutional management. This
accountability is increasingly delivered through the elaboration of internal
planning processes, often supported by rigorous financial arrangements,
such as an internal market between cost centres, or through the employment of techniques such as zero-based or priority-based budgeting. Such
developments make central departments such as the library accountable
both to faculties and to top management... Central departments in this situation are forced, whether they like it or not, to spend their money in a
way that meets with institutional approval. This accountability can be very
tangible, for example where a library has its budgets cut because it loses
the confidence of those to whom it is accountable. On the other hand,
libraries that secure strong support will probably attract additional
resources.

(Heery, 1993, p.139)

'Accountability' means that libraries are increasingly being held
accountable to both paymasters and users. Institutional executives
will want not only value for money from libraries, but also reassur-
ance that the library is working in support of institutional
objectives. Users – or customers, in the managerialist parlance – are
increasingly assertive about receiving a high quality, effective service from their library. These two areas of accountability are not of
course unrelated. The opinions about the library that are held by

staff and students will eventually influence the views of those who allocate resources.

The growing accountability of academic libraries should result in them becoming more concerned with the effectiveness of the service they offer. The 'reputation' of the library in the institution is important. Librarians need the political and negotiating skills that will win friends and influence the powerful. They need to be able to promote the library effectively. They also need to understand how the institution conducts itself, that is, its culture. Clearly it is inappropriate for the library to develop a highly quantitative approach to performance indicators if the institutional management has little interest in that approach. However, there is no escaping the fact that the reputation of the library rests primarily not upon the political effectiveness of the chief librarian, but on the quality of the service it provides. 'Accountability' inevitably means that the quality of library services (its outputs) are brought under scrutiny. Librarians need to know how effective their services are, and be able to convince those to whom they are accountable.

Comparative exercises

Considerable effort has been expended in trying to assess individual libraries by comparing them with others. For example, SCONUL has collected annual statistics about university libraries. The CVCP has identified a range of financial indicators for university libraries. This comparative approach to performance assessment is problematic. The intention may be straightforward – how does our library compare with others? – but it is difficult to achieve. Libraries vary considerably.

The CVCP approach has been criticized by Lines (1989) for being too FTE-oriented, at the expense of libraries with large research collections. Library statistics can be problematic because they are chiefly concerned with inputs, whereas it is the library's outputs that mostly need to be evaluated. Brophy (1989, p.103) has criticized the league tables that often result from such statistics:

if you are above the mean in terms of resources expended you will have to work very hard indeed to avoid cuts. . . . The lesson is perhaps to avoid the top half of the league table. But you can be equally assured that if you are operating below the mean resource level you will simply be heartily congratulated and told to carry on with the good work. Before we know where we are the mean will be treated as a *maximum*.

These external indicators will be viewed warily by the library manager. Comparison between libraries is hindered by the very different
nature of different libraries. Generic indicators are beset with difficulties. Quantifiable elements such as staff, budgets, buildings and
equipment may need to be quite different in, for example, a
multi-site library than in a single-site library. Different academic
libraries, for a whole host of reasons, will be pursuing different
strategies. Henty (1989, p.190) concludes that

all libraries should be responsible for evaluating their own services, but
this should be in terms of whether they meet the objectives set for them by
their parent body, not in terms of whether they meet externally set and possibly incompatible objectives imposed from outside.

The recent recommendations of the SCONUL Advisory
Committee on Performance Indicators are explored further in the
final chapter. These retain some quantitative measures of performance, which are considerably improved as they recommend
comparison between institutions of similar type. These criteria also
go some way towards identifying indicators that are sensitive to the
requirements of the library's parent body.

Quantitative measures

Some quantitative output measures will probably always be used to
assess libraries – the number of issues, interlibrary loans, user education sessions etc. – even though they are difficult to interpret.
Librarians will find ways of using such figures in the day to day business of negotiating with those to whom the library is accountable.
However, such data will do relatively little to inform the librarian
about how services should develop in response to a changing environment. It is often very difficult to know how to act upon the
statistics that are collected. They may record swings in the numbers
of those using the library, but they may contribute little to evaluating
the effectiveness of a particular service. How should we assess user
education, enquiry services, interlibrary loans or CD-ROM services?
It is necessary to get beyond the statistical data if by themselves they
cannot tell us what we need to know. As Cotta-Schonberg and Line
(1994, p.56) rightly point out, the opinions of users are a very important measure of how the library is performing.

Purely quantitative indicators are not by themselves adequate. The figures may be accurate as far as they go, but they are often based on samples or estimates, and they have an apparent precision which may be spurious. It is therefore important to complement them with qualitative indicators. . . . feelings about the library, whether justified nor not, are often as important as facts, sometimes more so when decisions come to be made about policy and funding.

Qualitative measures

From a management perspective the measurement of library performance via surveys of users may be very effective. Where results are favourable the information will be suitable for use within the institution, as it will be highly credible. The suspicion that sometimes greets the presentation of quantitative data will be absent where information is generated by high profile user surveys. Indeed, surveys can generate goodwill, in that the library is clearly taking an interest in the views of its clients. Computer-generated statistical data have little promotional value compared with direct contact with users. If possible, the library should try to participate in university-wide surveys so as to maximize opportunities for using the data that are collected. As Richard (1992, p.32) advises: 'Surveys of satisfaction should cover the whole institution, not just the library element, allowing the degree of satisfaction with the library to be put in the context of the whole institution's services'.

Quantitative and qualitative measures are compared and contrasted in Chapter 9.

The rich picture

In practice managers are likely to evaluate library services using a mix of assessments. Statistical data will be used where appropriate, though few academic libraries have access to more than very basic management information systems. User surveys should be conducted from time to time, taking care not to alienate users with an excess of questionnaires. Course management committees and the annual cycle of course monitoring and evaluation should provide useful opportunities for feedback about the library. At any one time small-scale evaluative exercises will be running in the library to check the effectiveness and/or the efficiency of specific services or procedures. All these assessments should be overlaid by continuous informal feedback from faculties and departments. The library should be continually promoting itself within the institution, and checking that it retains institutional support. The library manager will be concerned to gauge the reputation of the library, as well as to evaluate its services. The organizational structure of the library will therefore be highly relevant in assessing the library's performance. Where the library is organized so that staff are well integrated into the academic life of the institution there will be good opportunities for feedback about the library. As the library is providing a range of services, close contact with the users of those services will be an important precondition to effective assessment. If performance assessment is to be part of the day to day management of the library, and not an artificial add-on, the internal organization of the library needs to facilitate evaluative feedback from users. In assessing a library, therefore, it is important to decide whether its staff structure, its procedures and its links with the rest of the institution are such as to enable it to obtain relevant information from its users on a regular basis. Examples of useful links are attendance at course planning meetings, course management committees, and site user groups, as well as opportunities for day to day informal liaison with faculty staff. A snapshot of these kinds of activities in the further and higher education sectors is provided in the next chapter.

A mixed approach may appear somewhat unsystematic. However, this 'rich picture' approach is recognized as a legitimate form of performance assessment. It has been used to good effect by the library of the Royal Military College at Shrivenham, where a large-scale benchmarking exercise was used in the comparative evaluation of a number of academic libraries (Town, 1995). The 'rich picture' approach avoids over-reliance on systems of assessment which could disrupt the everyday work of the library. It is related to the structure of the library. It is also sensitive to the views of library staff. It is very important to involve library staff in performance assessment. This point is emphasized by Abbott (1994, p.38): 'The development of performance indicators should not be seen as isolated from the normal process of management, nor should they be developed by one person, single-handed'. If staff are not to feel threatened by performance assessment it must be seen to be demonstrably of use to the day to day work of library staff. It should not impose an additional burden of further work without the support of staff. Indeed, the workload imposed by performance assessment is something managers must consider carefully when deciding what to do.

The evaluation effort needs to pay for itself in more effective and efficient operations. This was confirmed at the University of Houston, where, after eight years, their system of efficiency evaluation began to cost very little less than the savings achieved, so it was determined the effort was better placed in providing services than evaluating costs. This indicates that the system of performance indicators needs to be monitored in the same way as other activities.

(Richard, 1992, p.26)

The management of performance assessment requires that managers use their judgement to ensure that evaluation is useful to the development of the library and that it also fits well into the overall management style.

CONCLUSIONS

Morgan's (1993) survey of academic librarians has shown that relatively few conduct systematic performance assessment. It is often regarded as too time consuming and has a low priority. There may be some uncertainty of definition behind these findings. However, the aim of this chapter is to show that those managing academic libraries should accept the usefulness of managerial skills such as strategic planning. If they do so, performance assessment will naturally become part of how they decide whether or not they are achieving their objectives. However conscious library managers are of concepts such as managerialism, growing accountability to those who allocate institutional resources should result in a real concern for the quality of library services. It is the author's belief that the application of 'common sense and conventional wisdom' (McLean and Wilde, 1991, p.210) to the performance assessment process can result from a new understanding of managerialism in the workplace, and from appreciation of how performance assessment relates to organizational structure.

The purpose of performance assessment must always be borne in mind. 'It is to answer questions that need answering, whether to satisfy the librarian's need to know how efficiently his or her library runs, or to satisfy the library's management committee or funding body', as Cotta-Schonberg and Line (1994, p.55) rightly state. Librarians will often know from their experience what questions need answering. However, day to day pressures, together with problems inherent in assessing educational services, will make the provision of easy answers difficult. It is often difficult to interpret findings, or to know how to act on them. Yet the need to offer evidence of effective performance is inescapable. Librarians need to organize their libraries so that they are closely attuned to the needs of their institutions.

Performance assessment requires integration with the users of the library. It also requires the integration of management with library staff. If performance assessment is to be effective in a public service environment the managerial approach needs to be based on a relationship of trust with employees. We need to get rid of simplistic, top-down notions of evaluation. Flynn has provided a succinct summary of the task now facing library managers: 'Performance measurement must be transformed into a positive device for communicating with service users and for demonstrating and celebrating success as well as for exposing and correcting shortcomings' (Flynn, 1993, p.200).

FURTHER READING

Butler, M. and Davis, H. (1992) 'Strategic planning as a catalyst for change in the 1990s.' *College and Research Libraries* **53**(5), 393–403.

Farnham, D. and Horton, S. (eds.) (1993) *Managing the New Public Services*. London: Macmillan.

Line, M. (1991) 'Library management styles and structures: a need to rethink?' *Journal of Librarianship and Information Science* **23**(2), 97–104

McKevitt, D. and Lawton, A. (eds.) (1994) *Public Sector Management: Theory, Critique and Practice*. London: Sage.

Open University (1991) *B887 Managing Public Services*. Milton Keynes: Open University Press.

Pollitt, C. and Harrison, S. (1992) *Handbook of Public Services Management*. Oxford: Blackwell.

CHAPTER FOUR

The library perspective

An objective measure is the number of boxes of biscuits,
chocolates and bottles of wine brought in by departing students:
on this basis our performance leaves nothing to be desired!
(HE College Librarian)

It [the Government focusing on the FE sector] certainly will
shake up a few librarians from their slumbers and make them
realise that they too are accountable.
(FE College Librarian)

The issues addressed in this chapter are:

- the nature and extent of performance assessment activity in further education libraries
- the nature and extent of performance assessment activity in higher education libraries;
- themes that are common to both sectors;

It is quite possible to form a distorted and somewhat inflated view of the developments taking place within the academic library world through reading the appropriate professional literature. Because a handful of projects are reportedly taking place in one sector – let us say concerning cooperative cataloguing or information skills teaching or document availability surveys – one may believe mistakenly that such levels of activity are representative of the sector as a whole.

Alongside the rhetoric versus reality problem a number of other reasons have emerged for exploring the nature and extent of performance assessment activity in the academic sector. First, whilst the increase in student numbers within higher education has temporarily abated (Feather and Marriott, 1993), the Government has now focused its attention on the further education sector. Incorporation of the polytechnics at the end of the last decade was followed in April 1993 by that of the FE colleges. Such independence has highlighted the importance of ensuring that the standards of course/programme delivery and support services remain high and that the students' needs are adequately met. These moves coupled with the blurring of the higher education binary divide in 1992 have created a competitive educational environment for the post-16 student group. The FE sector is seen as a vital factor in not only contributing to the provision of a highly skilled workforce but also in acting as a channel for increased access to higher education. This view is reflected in the Government's policy to achieve 25% growth in the sector by 1996 (Further Education Funding Council, 1993). Greater independence has also highlighted other concerns which up until recently have been features of the private sector, such as greater accountability, value for money, responding to the needs of customers, issues of quality and performance etc. Just how far some of these issues have been addressed is unknown.

Second, most academic librarians would consider it important to know how well libraries in their particular sector are performing and therefore be able to place their own progress (or otherwise) in context. Similarly and more importantly, they would wish to gauge the library's performance in relation to their own aims and objectives and those of the parent organization. This was a point emphasized by the Joint Funding Councils' Libraries Review Group (1993, p.32): 'performance indicators should be related to the aims of the individual institutions, and within these, to those of the library'. Third, knowledge about the activities of other institutions may provide a potential plethora of ideas for libraries to take up.

In order to find out what kinds of activities have been taking place in recent times, two postal surveys were carried out – one for each of the sectors (see Appendices I and II for questionnaires). In this chapter the results of the surveys and their implications are explored, together with discussion of some themes common to both.

FURTHER EDUCATION SECTOR

To place the library service in context within this sector and address specific issues including current learning processes and the librarian's role in it, quality and resources, the book by Adams and

McElroy (1994) is a recommended up-to-date source.

As Salter (1993) correctly states, the further education sector has long been overshadowed by its better resourced partner. An example of this can be seen at the COFHE Conference in 1988 concerning evaluation of library services at which all the speakers were HE library practitioners.

The FEFC has responsibility for the 465 FE institutions (this figure includes specialist, tertiary and sixth form colleges) which provide educational services to over two million students (800 000 FTE). The diversity of the institutions in this sector is reflected in the varied nature of the curricula. These include foundation, general, vocational and adult education programmes; specialist short courses; higher education programmes sometimes offered on a franchised basis in collaboration with an HE institution; open and distance learning programmes; access programmes for mature students who wish to gain entry into higher education; and a wide range of general studies programmes, college societies and clubs aimed at broadening the students' education and training base. Since most college students are aiming for a national qualification, examining and validating bodies have a significant influence on the development of FE curricula.

So what has actually been happening in this sector in relation to performance assessment in libraries/resource centres? The main objectives of the survey were to find out:

- how committed further education institutions are to the assessment of their library services;
- how committed the libraries themselves are to the assessment of their performance;
- the extent of recent reader services evaluation and the methods used (the reader services alluded to here are those considered in Chapters 5, 6 and 7);
- how libraries collect feedback from their users about service provision;
- satisfaction levels of library managers with current assessment procedures;
- the views of library managers on assessment procedures in their own institutions or the wider further education sector.

To gather this information a questionnaire (see Appendix I) was sent to a random selection of colleges. These institutions were taken from Recurrent Funding Allocations to the FEFC Sector Colleges

1994/95 (*Times Higher Education Supplement*, 10 June 1994). Of the 290 available colleges (excluding sixth form colleges and specialist institutions such as agricultural, horticultural and art colleges), 200 were surveyed. Responses were received from 130 although 7 were unusable. The final usable responses rate (61.5%) was sufficient to provide a fairly reliable snapshot of activity across the sector as a whole.

Written Institutional Commitment

Responses suggested that around a third (34.2%) of the parent organizations had a written commitment to assessing their library's performance (Table 4.1). Indeed, six respondents identified the lack of commitment on the part of the institution's senior management to the library generally as a major problem. The following quote sums up the feelings of these respondents:

I do not think our college library is alone in having a higher management which undervalues the library service and until their attitude changes we face an uphill battle getting them to take seriously anything that the library tries to do.

Table 4.1 Further education sector: library commitment

	YES	NO
Written institutional commitment	42 (34.2%)	81 (65.8%)
Written library policy	32 (26%)	91 (74%)
Both	25 (20.3%)	
Neither	75 (61%)	

Mention was also made of colleges' involvement in quality assurance programmes including BS5750 accreditation and wider Total Quality Management (TQM) initiatives. A handful indicated that their library's services were evaluated either as part of a college-wide quality system (run by a Quality Unit, Quality Panel or other similarly named body). Depending on the degree of cooperation between the central and library services, this can be a two-edged sword. On the one hand it may provide the opportunity for a more integrated approach to service evaluation and lend more credibility to the outcome, but on the other hand it may reflect a lack of understanding on the part of the central administration of what actually goes on in the library.

A postal survey (Sallis 1990) was carried out to gauge the extent of the quality initiatives taking place in the sector. Around 180 indicated that they were aiming at BS5750 accreditation or some TQM-type approach. This survey would suggest that intentions at the beginning of the decade have subsequently been watered down. A recent survey (Utley 1994) suggested that FE colleges have rejected the quality standard (4% said that they were committed to it) in favour of the Investors in People initiative (79% were aiming for this). The difficulty of applying the standard in an educational context was offered as the major reason for rejection.

Six respondents stated that library reader services were evaluated as part of a wider annual survey to gauge student satisfaction with all the support services.

Written Library Policy

Ninety-one of the responding libraries (74%) had no written policies on evaluating their own services (Table 4.1). Seven libraries indicated that such a document was in preparation. Twelve libraries recognized the importance of the FEFC inspections taking place throughout the sector. Following the Further and Higher Education Act (1992) the FEFC has a duty to ensure that satisfactory arrangements exist to assess the quality of education provided in colleges within the sector. As part of this external assessment the FEFC inspection teams plan to visit all the FE colleges at least once every four years (this process began in Autumn 1993). These teams assess the different curriculum areas and cross-college aspects of provision including responsiveness and range of provision; governance and management; student recruitment, guidance and support; quality assurance; and resources (including libraries/resource centres). An assessment grade is then assigned to each aspect/curriculum area on a scale of 1 (many strengths, few weaknesses) to 5 (many weaknesses, few strengths). Interviews with FEFC personnel by Bibby *et al*. (1994) indicated that the Inspectorate would be looking at the following areas:

- Book and periodical collections – Are they up-to-date? Is there under or over supply?
- Number of sites – What relationship exists between them? What networks are there between sites, for example, catalogues?
- Quality of catalogues, handouts, help given.
- Staffing levels – Are they term-time only?
- Opening hours – Are they appropriate?
- Specialist provision – CD-ROM, computer facilities, audio-visual material.
- Security systems.
- Study rooms/areas – Are they appropriate and accessible?
- The broad ethos of the library: the subtle difference between a place where students want to work or want to leave as soon as possible.

Further Education Funding Council (1993) is an important circular which sets out a proposed framework for inspection. Provision of resources and the support available to students are addressed in this document. It seems that these inspections are acting as a motivating force in at least prompting the library to consider a more systematic approach to service evaluation. One library had established a working party consisting of a group of local college librarians who were setting out guidelines for self-inspection prior to FEFC visits 'to try and avoid pitfalls'. One FE librarian (Davies, 1994) has taken an interesting further step by becoming a lay inspector with the FEFC. He detailed the training undertaken and views the prospects of college libraries within the new scenario.

Such forward-looking approaches are to be applauded. An opposing view was expressed, however, by a significant minority of respondents who were waiting for the FEFC to lay down its own national standards on performance assessment or at least sets of performance criteria. This may yet be some way off.

The issue of library versus institutional control of the assessment process arises again. Responses suggested a certain ambivalence about the issue, but a recognition of both the benefits of dovetailing into the parent organization's mission and strategy and also the importance of the librarian's independence and control in formulating suitable policies within the institutional framework. As one respondent put it: 'The evaluation process . . . is always a highly politicised area and I feel sometimes I would rather retain control of it within the library service'.

The excellent document produced under the chairmanship of Burness (Burness, 1993) reviewed the role of the FE College Libraries in Scotland and offered some valuable recommendations including seeing performance assessment as a dual commitment:

We recommend that, as part of their overall quality programme, colleges monitor library quality and performance to ensure that the college is resourcing the library adequately to meet the demand placed upon it and that these resources are being used well by librarians. There is a dual commitment: the library should seek to improve service and efficiency; college management should respond to the resource and organisational implications of performance data

(Paragraph 121)

Twenty-five (20.3%) of the respondents had written commitments to library service assessment at the level of both the institution and the library. Not surprisingly, such commitment was reflected both in the variety of reader service evaluation taking place in these libraries and also in the different channels through which user feedback was sought. Conversely, 75 (61%) libraries showed written commitment at neither institutional nor library levels. The reader service evaluation and feedback activities followed no general pattern in these libraries.

Reader Services

For the purposes of this survey it was decided to concentrate on those reader services which were recognized in the literature as being the main ones (see later in this chapter). The opportunity was given to indicate any other reader services that were assessed and these are covered below.

A small number of respondents (5.7%) indicated that they evaluated all the reader services on offer. Incidentally, five out of seven had parent institutions which had a written commitment to assessing the library's performance. Conversely, nearly one in three (37 libraries) had not assessed any of its reader services. Rather worryingly, four out of the 37 expressed their satisfaction with current assessment procedures. These results are summarized in Table 4.2.

Table 4.2 Further education libraries: reader services

Assessable elements	No. of institutions (%)
Book/periodical usage	74 (60.2%)
Book/periodical availability	26 (21.1%)
Book reservations	23 (18.7%)
Interlibrary loan requests	23 (18.7%)
Readers' enquiries	30 (24.4%)
User education	42 (34.2%)
Others	27 (22%)
All reader services	7 (5.7%)
No reader services	37 (30.1%)

Book and Periodical Usage

Book usage (60.2%) was by far the most evaluated of the services. However, such evaluation was restricted mainly to computer transaction (or manually derived) statistics rather than any kind of qualitative process, as described in Chapter 5. Certainly some responses indicated that computerized systems might be generating reports which contained more sophisticated information on usage by certain groups of certain types of material. Responses such as 'data from computerised library system', 'reports generated by the system', 'MIS and checking items on shelves' and 'statistics from management system' provide no evidence as to how automated systems were being used for this purpose.

Evaluation of periodicals usage was carried out by far fewer libraries (8.1%). Attaching a slip of paper to the front of each periodical was the most favoured approach, together with a request not to reshelve the periodicals (for a specific period of time) so that usage could be marked off on a list.

Book and Periodical Availability

According to the survey, availability studies which are explored in more depth in Chapter 5 have been carried out recently by 26 (21.1%) of the libraries, mainly through user surveys. Salter (1993; 1994) describes a document availability study carried out in Acton

College Library which concentrated particularly on the needs of Advanced Level and access course students who rely heavily on reading lists. It would be less appropriate for BTEC students, for example, whose needs are usually for information rather than textbooks. The current survey showed no specific examples of periodical availability studies.

Reservation and Interlibrary Loan Services
In each of these categories, 23 respondents (18.7%) answered that they evaluated these services principally in terms of turnaround time or, in the case of reservations, 'requested materials delay', as Van House *et al.* (1990) term it. Some libraries indicated that they made very little use of the British Library's Document Supply Service since costs are prohibitively high. Cooperation with local public library services takes place on a fairly modest scale. The interlibrary loan service of one college library had been evaluated recently in terms of running costs.

Readers' Enquiries
As Chapter 7 demonstrates, the literature on this complex area is quite extensive. Much of the research has taken place in the US, although Williams' work (Williams, 1987) in a London polytechnic is still interesting and worth reading. No substantial research has been carried out on evaluation of enquiry services in the FE sector.

According to the survey nearly a quarter of the respondents (30 libraries) evaluated this particular service. Most of the methods used were quantitative. Those mentioned were 'count within broad categories', 'unanswered query slips', 'diary log' and 'monitoring sheets'. Seven colleges recently carried out surveys to gauge the effectiveness of enquiry services.

User Education
After book usage, user education (34.2%) was the most heavily evaluated of the reader services. These 42 libraries employed a mixture of surveying individuals via questionnaires following teaching sessions and feedback from course review meetings. The FE sector has a long tradition of concentration on information, communication and study skills. This approach has been driven partly by the professional and vocational bodies, which stipulate the skills required for success, and partly through the highlighting of competencies (as in GNVQs). The move towards a more student-centred approach,

which predated the move in the higher education sector, through resource-based learning has necessitated ensuring that the students become more self-reliant particularly in the sphere of familiarity with information technology and associated skills. This is an area of further education about which much research work has been done in recent years. Morrison (1991), Markless and Streatfield (1992) and Morrison and Markless (1992) have provided a comprehensive set of reports on information skills teaching, culminating in a set of recommendations for a more coherent and consistent approach.

The survey suggests that there is now greater convergence between library and teaching staff in many colleges. This is manifested in a greater involvement in:

- course and curriculum planning;
- task groups;
- monitoring, evaluation and quality issues;
- writing of working papers;
- appointment of subject librarians or resource-based learning coordinators (the nomenclature varies) to act in a liaising and teaching capacity;
- joint planning agreements or strategic plans.

From personal experience of teaching information-handling skills to access and franchise students, the author is generally heartened by the study skills and general awareness demonstrated within a sometimes intimidating higher education library environment. This is partly a testament to the effective programmes of study delivered at local colleges and partly down to the motivation and enthusiasm of the students.

Other Reader Services

Respondents were invited to include other reader services which had been evaluated over the previous year. These services were computing facilities including CD-ROM databases, OPACs, audiovisual and illustration collections and reprographics facilities.

Feedback from Users

As discussed in Chapter 2, it is vital that the views of the service's users are sought to help inform the debate about the library's performance. From a variety of vehicles that are available to gain feedback the survey included four, with the option of including

others if necessary. The results of the survey with regard to feedback
are summarized in Table 4.3.

Table 4.3 Further education libraries: feedback channels

Feedback channel	Number of institutions (%)
Monitoring and evaluation	72 (58.5%)
Discussion groups	25 (20.3%)
Satisfaction surveys	70 (56.9%)
Informal discussion	85 (69.1%)
Other	22 (17.9%)
No feedback	11 (8.9%)

Informal discussion (69.1%) was the most frequently cited means
of seeking feedback on service provision. A handful of respondents
indicated that the informal discussions took place with academic
staff and course tutors.

Monitoring and evaluation of teaching programmes was mentioned by 72 (58.5%) libraries as one channel of feedback. This
feedback was referred to under a range of names including 'course
review meetings' and 'student representatives on course committees'. Such channels were considered useful for broad-brush views
of library performance or for highlighting particular courses/subject
areas with significant deficiencies. They also provided the opportunity for the service to be the object of praise!

Satisfaction surveys (56.9%) came a close second in citation
terms. Such surveys were often carried out as part of a college-wide
exercise which included the support services. These exercises
involved 'customer service unit', 'college marketing office', 'general interviews', 'exit (leaving college) survey' and 'general
questionnaire'. On the other hand some libraries took responsibility
themselves and sought views on the service in a more detailed and
specific way.

Around one in five respondents (25 libraries) used formal discussion groups to glean the views of the service users. These took the
form of 'user groups' whose *raison d'être* was to provide feedback
to the library in a representative and structured way. Under this

heading one could also place 'library committee' and 'IT and resources committee'.

Whilst the twenty-two libraries (17.9%) which mentioned other feedback methods were indicating variations on the above themes, the only ones that did not fall into any of these categories were suggestions and complaints (via books, cards or boxes). Ten libraries referred to these methods, and opinions tended to be divided on their usefulness. Were they merely a public relations exercise? Were they one part of a customer care approach? Were the suggestions ever acted upon? Did the authors of suggestions receive replies? Was the book/box prominently placed or hidden away? Were users generally encouraged to make use of it? Perhaps these methods are best used as an adjunct to the assessment of library service quality to provide a more rounded picture.

Finally, eleven of the respondents sought no feedback from users at all.

Satisfaction with Current Procedures

Attitude measurement is an inexact science (Oppenheim, 1992), in particular with regard to the difficulty of comparability of respondents' opinions and varying levels of expectation. This latter point is discussed in Chapter 2. However, satisfaction levels can act as a broad indicator.

Table 4.4 Further education libraries: satisfaction levels

Level of satisfaction	Number of institutions (%)
Very satisfied	5 (4.3%)
Satisfied	24 (20.5%)
Not very satisfied	67 (57.3%)
Dissatisfied	21 (18%)

* 6 gave no opinion

The results of the survey indicated that about a quarter of the libraries (29) were satisfied or very satisfied with their performance assessment procedures whilst the other 88 showed varying degrees of dissatisfaction. The five libraries which expressed the highest degree of satisfaction with procedures all had written performance assessment policies at the levels of both the parent institution and the library. These results are summarized in Table 4.4.

General Comments

Most of the comments made by responding librarians have been included at appropriate points in the survey discussion. The most consistently cited comments were concerned with lack of time and resources for staff to carry out assessment of the library service. The following quotations give a flavour of their feelings:

> 'Performing at all is the problem'.
> 'Survival seems more important than quality of service'.
> 'In the present climate we are running to stand still'.

A handful of respondents indicated that such service assessment was not a current priority. Perhaps this is reflected by the librarian who wrote 'we all know or have got feelings about what is a good service'. The discussions in Chapter 2 suggest that there are difficulties with subjective judgements of what constitutes 'goodness'. It may also be an excuse for inertia.

HIGHER EDUCATION SECTOR

As has already been mentioned in relation to the FE sector, it is difficult to gauge by reading the literature the nature and extent of performance assessment activity taking place within the higher education sector. With UK student numbers having increased by a massive 70% over the last six years, it is essential that mechanisms are in place to monitor and evaluate the library services so that the highest standards of provision are maintained. The students have a right to expect certain standards of quality and service in the education they experience. The continuous driving down of the unit of resource further emphasizes the importance of achieving value for money within the learning support services as in any other department.

The literature also has little to report on performance assessment activity within the reader services which for the purposes of this survey are defined as:

- provision of book and periodical collections;
- provision of a readers' enquiry service;
- teaching of information-handling skills.

So what has actually been happening in the libraries of the higher education sector and are there differences between the 'old' and 'new' universities and the HE colleges? The main objectives of the survey were to find out:

- how committed the HE institutions are to the assessment of their library service;
- how committed the libraries themselves are to the assessment of their performance;
- the extent of reader services evaluation, the methods used to evaluate and the groups consulted;
- which groups received the results of any evaluation process over the previous year;
- satisfaction levels of library managers with current assessment procedures where they existed and how these might be improved.

A postal questionnaire (see Appendix II) was sent to 119 HE libraries comprising those of 50 'old' and 40 'new' universities together with 29 colleges. The final usable responses (78) were sufficient in both absolute terms (66%) and across the three erstwhile sectors (62%, 70%, 66% respectively) to provide a reliable snapshot of performance assessment activity.

Written Institutional Commitment

Responses suggested that just over a third (35.9%) of the parent organizations had a written commitment to assessing their library's performance (Table 4.5). Documents in which performance criteria were included were called variously 'mission statements', 'aims and objectives', 'internal academic audit group statement', 'strategic plan', 'development plan' and 'approvals and reviews committee statement'. One University produced an interesting response: 'insufficient institutional pressure to produce written policy statements (ethos of institution)'. From comments received from a number of libraries it appeared that performance assessment was currently in the process of being addressed but had not yet been translated into written commitments.

Table 4.5 Higher education sector: library commitment

	YES	NO
Written institutional commitment	28 (35.9%)	50 (64.1%)
Written library policy	24 (30.8%)	54 (69.2%)
Both	15 (19.2%)	
Neither	40 (51.3%)	

Written Library Policy

Twenty-four (30.8%) of the libraries had written policies on assessment of the library service (Table 4.5); of these only five were from the 'old' university sector. Many different reasons were put forward by the library managers for having no written policy, but the reasons tended to fall into three categories: policy documents currently under development; insufficient time or staff; library policy unnecessary. Three of the 'new' universities suggested such policies were unnecessary since assessment was 'implicit in everything we do'. One respondent put it thus: 'We assume to run and manage the library with quality of service constantly assessed'. One university referred to the lack of research on measures of library quality commenting that 'we tend not to have written policies and the argument is that there aren't valid performance indicators particularly for qualitative aspects of service'.

Fifteen (19.2%) libraries had written commitments at the level of both the institution and the library. Conversely, of the forty without a written commitment at either level, nineteen were from the 'old' university sector.

Reader Services

For the purposes of the survey reader services (Table 4.6) were divided into three areas:

- *Document Provision:* book collections (availability and usage); periodical collections (availability and usage); interlibrary loan services (turnaround time); book reservations (turnaround time).
- *Readers' Enquiries:* the face to face enquiry interviews in which users require a service over and above the use of the library for studying or for the issue/return of books.
- *User Education:* the imparting of library and information skills by library staff to users in formal group work or classroom settings.

Table 4.6 Higher education libraries: reader services

Assessable elements	Number of institutions (%)
Book collections	39 (50%)
Periodical collections	40 (51.3%)
Interlibrary loan services	25 (32.1%)
Book reservations	21 (26.9%)
Readers' enquiries	19 (24.4%)
User education	36 (46.2%)
All reader services	2 (2.6%)
No reader services	12 (15.4%)

Book and Periodical Collections

The figures showed that in both areas around a half of the libraries had carried out some kind of evaluation within the previous year. For book collections the main methods were user surveys (19 libraries), evaluation by academic staff and/or subject librarians (8 libraries) and quantification by computer system (8 libraries). For periodical collections user surveys (20 libraries) and departmental reviews (7 libraries) were favoured. Rather more activity took place in the 'old' university sector, possibly reflecting not only their higher levels of spending on periodical literature to support institutional research, but also the increasing costs of individual subscriptions. (In the UK average periodical subscription prices have increased by 85% since 1988, according to the Library and Information Statistics Unit.)

Interlibrary Loan and Reservation Services
Both of these services were evaluated in terms of speed of delivery by under a third of the libraries (26.9%). The 'new' universities were the most proactive on both counts. The main reasons given for non-assessment of document provision overall were low priority, insufficient time or staff and pressure of other work.

Readers' Enquiry Service
Around three-quarters of the libraries (57) indicated that their enquiry services were not evaluated in any way. Of the nineteen which did, fifteen were universities. The methods of evaluation were user surveys and observation by library staff. The reasons for non-assessment were generally similar to those previously mentioned, together with the difficulty of assessing the quality of such interactions. This problem is highlighted in Chapter 7.

User Education
Just under a half of the libraries (36) assessed their user education programmes, with the 'new' universities being the most active sector. Many polytechnics traditionally had well-developed user education programmes (Cowley and Hammond, 1987; Fletcher, 1985). This tradition was partly explained by the fact that their degree courses had to be approved by the Council for National Academic Awards (CNAA). Their subject expert panels insisted that a certain number of hours of user education be incorporated into courses. User surveys, observation and interviews were used for evaluation purposes.

Whilst only two libraries carried out some evaluation of all the reader services outlined in the survey, a fairly substantial number (12) did none at all, even though two of these indicated that they had a written commitment to performance assessment!

Dissemination of Results

Forty-five libraries (57.7%) presented their results to people or bodies outside of the immediate library environment as well as using them for in-house purposes. The two main bodies to receive results were library committees (28) and the senior management of the institutions (24). Interestingly only 13 libraries fed their results back to the main users of the service – the students.

Satisfaction with Current Procedures

Whilst recognizing the difficulties of attitude measurement, it can serve as a guide to general feelings and perceptions of the library managers. The satisfaction level across the university and college sectors may be described as 4 on a scale of 1 (totally dissatisfied) to 10 (very satisfied). Such a low overall level and the responses from the librarians would suggest that many wished to improve the process, and indeed put forward ideas for doing so.

Improvement of Assessment Procedures

Suggested improvements could be divided into the five broad areas described below.

1. Greater involvement of library staff and users
This involvement could include a more widespread adoption of user satisfaction surveys (mentioned by 12 libraries).

2. More systematic, structured and holistic approach
According to a number of libraries their performance assessment activities were carried out on an *ad hoc* basis, for example, using small samples for specific subject areas or evaluating one part of the service when required. Regular evaluation using standardized and consistent techniques with a basket of measures was recommended (see Chapter 10 for progress by the SCONUL group). One of the problems is deciding what to include in the basket. Cotta-Schonberg and Line (1994) have addressed this very issue in a Business School Library in the Netherlands.

3. Specialist staff
A handful of librarians suggested the employment of specialist staff to assist in the assessment process. This move could prove effective as long as staff with the necessary skills and expertise – librarianship? research methods? psychology? education? – could be either recruited or trained. One university suggested calling on the expertise of academic departments for this purpose. One also put forward the idea of setting up a review of its library service with assessors from other libraries and institutional academic staff – a kind of peer review system.

4. More effective use of computer systems

All libraries in higher education nowadays possess automated systems for an increasing number of library activities. Many of these systems have the capability of providing ever more sophisticated management information. From comments received from library managers it is clear that many libraries do not use these systems to the full, possibly for the reasons already stated – lack of priority, lack of staff, lack of time and, perhaps, lack of funds.

5. More time

This plea was made by ten respondents. They felt that the pressures of providing the services themselves to ever greater numbers of users left them with little time to devote to assessing the performance of such services. However, one university librarian added a note of caution 'not to spend so much time measuring how we do the job that we detract from our performance'.

COMMON THEMES

Although academic libraries in the context of this book consist of those in further and higher education, it is worth dwelling briefly on the enormous diversity of provision along this spectrum. At the one end you will find the tertiary college with perhaps 5000 books and a handful of periodical subscriptions. Its computing facilities may be basic, it may be staffed by a recently qualified librarian and have very little institutional support. At the other end you will find the traditional university library with perhaps copyright deposit, generously resourced in bookstock, computer facilities and staffing. This library will be fully integrated into the strategic planning, development and evaluation processes taking place in the parent institution. Similarly, some FE college libraries may be better resourced in terms of physical material (books and equipment) and staffing than some HE colleges. Bibby et al. (1994) provide statistics on the preincorporation FE sector, particularly on resourcing and staffing.

Such scenarios, however, are not enlightening in terms of the quality of the service provision. Indeed it is possible that the apparently down-at-heel college library may provide a more effective service than the apparently opulent university library. In the former case the librarian may argue that the financial constraints under which the library operates make it imperative that the funding is spent wisely. The librarian may have taken the time and trouble to find out the needs of the students and staff and to tailor the service accordingly – the right books and periodical subscriptions easily located, the required IT facilities, a good relationship with curriculum leaders and corresponding tightly focused user education, enthusiastically and effectively delivered.

Conversely the university library may purchase single copies of most titles; may provide limited user education programmes for effective retrieval, evaluation and use of material via printed and electronic sources; may offer limited networking and other IT facilities; may staff the enquiry desks with subject 'specialists' who have little control over selection or funding and may not attend appropriate departmental forums for liaison purposes.

Without labouring the point further and recognizing that there are extreme cases, the surveys suggest that such pictures are not wildly inaccurate in a small minority of libraries. Therefore, for the majority, it is not surprising that the gulf between the two sectors in assessing library performance is fairly narrow in terms of written policy commitment and, to a lesser degree, in terms of reader services activity. The commitment to performance assessment through written policies (institutional and library) is similar across the sectors with around one third of institutions having produced such policies.

The level of activity within the HE library reader services is greater overall but not significantly so, as Tables 4.1 to 4.6 show. Against a background of concentrated government attention to a rising student population, more non-traditional students and a heavy reliance on independent study, two particular themes arise out of the surveys: first, the difficulty of collecting and interpreting qualitative data and, second, the motivational force of external assessment. There is also a common factor connecting these themes – a lack of time.

Qualitative Data

One of the main reasons that Chapter 9 concentrates more on questionnaires, interviews and discussion groups is the importance attached to these so called 'softer' or qualitative data by the survey respondents. Here are some comments to give a flavour of the feelings:

> ... anxious to improve qualitative feedback on services

rooted in specific information-seeking transactions.

Qualitative data is time consuming and difficult.

I have designed a form where the intention is to get responses from students about the usefulness of individual books – did it help/make a difference?

Librarians often seem to get hung up on figures; there is good reason to develop quality-based assessments.

We have tried to use instruments which assess satisfaction levels but have found the responses to be ambiguous.

A number of respondents mentioned that desirability for qualitative assessment was countered by the disproportionate amount of staff (or graduate, researcher etc) hours required to carry it out.

External Assessment

Both sectors are heavily influenced by their respective Funding Councils but particularly by visits or inspections. A number of libraries, especially in the FE sector, are heavily motivated to explore performance assessment when an inspection is imminent. It comes higher on the list of priorities and time has to be allocated to the establishment of appropriate procedures. The inspecting representatives of the Higher Education Funding Councils and those of the Higher Education Quality Council (HEQC) visit their institutions to examine quality assurance mechanisms and also the teaching and learning within individual subject areas. The learning support services are checked out during an inspection and both types of occasion provide the library with the opportunity to ensure appropriate performance assessment activities are in place and functioning effectively. In each sector, whether as the initial motivating force behind the establishment of assessment systems or merely in the fine-tuning of existing ones, clearly such external bodies have an important role to play in this regard.

Perhaps there are reasons for remaining optimistic about the ability of both sectors to address performance assessment issues. In the HE sector the SCONUL group working on performance indicators shows no sign of flagging in its determination to establish appropriate measures. These points are picked up again and reinforced in Chapter 10 when looking to the future. The difficulties of assessing performance in terms of the needs of the research community may produce a more protracted discussion. In the FE sector, the Council for Learning Resources in Colleges (CoLRiC) was founded during 1993 as an independent support agency to libraries. Part of its remit is to set up performance indicators to assess efficiency and effectiveness in the sector's library services by mediating between the colleges and bodies such as the FEFC and the Department for Education.

CHAPTER FIVE

Book and periodical collections

No single technique may be regarded as adequate for complete
evaluation purposes, nor does the whole range of techniques
available provide any certainty of arriving at measures of collection adequacy which may be asserted irrefutable.

(Wainwright and Dean, 1976, p.82)

The issues addressed in this chapter are:

- the evaluation of collections in terms of quality and relevance;
- the availability of books and periodicals;
- the accessibility of books and periodicals;
- the use made of books and periodical collections.

Developments in information technology have been taking place
on a number of fronts. Networking (local, national and international) is now firmly rooted in the academic community:
CD-ROMs, other databases via JANET and soon SUPERJANET,
and the all-pervading Internet. The facility to send material via electronic mail has been in place for a while and continues to improve in
sophistication. Full-text databases and electronic journals have
become more widespread whilst standardization of interfaces
between systems brings the virtual library closer to reality.

To many of those students currently working their way through
post-compulsory education courses the above developments may
appear to reside in the realms of fantasy. They may see such developments as, at best, peripheral in their continuous striving to
prepare for the next seminar or beat the deadline for the next assignment. To them the discussion about the role of academic libraries as
points of access rather than collection builders is a sterile one. User
surveys undertaken at Sheffield Hallam, the University of Central

England and the University of Leicester have indicated recently that the concerns of students centre on the library's bookstock – adequacy, range, availability, up-to-dateness, numbers of copies etc.

As information technology developments play a more integral role in the provision of information services, so the users will become more proficient in manipulating the sources and the results. Training will take place through various means, for example, user education, individual tuition, workshops for academic staff – but in reality users will become aware of and knowledgeable about these facilities and services as they perceive the need arising. For some, the electronically aware, this process could be fairly short. Whilst the route for the students has often in the past been through the academic staff, nowadays one hears more and more of the reverse being the case. For others, the electronically apprehensive, the process could take a little longer.

Whilst the above paints a rather simplistic picture of undergraduate library use one recognizes that the library's clientele is far from being one homogeneous group. The needs of groups and, indeed, individuals vary. Some courses will require students to utilize information retrieval skills of a higher order for project or group work, particularly in the latter stages of undergraduate programmes. Equally, the nature of postgraduate and research programmes may demand that students equip themselves with the transferable skills necessary to satisfy their information needs. Such skills will inevitably involve the structured use of information technology. The researcher may also benefit from the breadth of subject coverage in the university library's book and periodical collections. Thus we return to the access versus collection-building debate, variously known as ephemeral versus eternal (Line, 1990) or just-in-time versus just-in-case (Morley and Woodward, 1993)

This preamble points to the importance which is still placed on the book and periodical collections by the users of the service. In the 1990s in most academic libraries these collections represent the backbone of the service and therefore libraries' strategic aims and objectives often revolve around provision, exploitation, development and monitoring of such collections. During the current decade identifying the precise purpose of these collections becomes a more difficult task since the balance between satisfying the needs of research and teaching varies from institution to institution. For a number of years the establishment of short loan or undergraduate collections have been viewed as a way of separating the two – teach-

ing and research. The argument that much of the research feeds into
the teaching programmes merely clouds an already complex issue.

Given the value placed upon book and periodical collections and
the amount of the library's budget spent on them it may come as a
surprise that only around a half of higher education libraries undertake any evaluation of their collections (Morgan 1993). Of the
expenditure within academic libraries during 1992/93, 32% was
spent on books and periodicals, according to the Library and
Information Statistics Unit. The reasons given by librarians for not
undertaking an evaluation were low priority, insufficient time or
staff and pressure of other work.

SO WHY EVALUATE COLLECTIONS?

The main purpose of evaluating the collections is to find out
whether the library is achieving its objectives and satisfying its
users' needs. Collection evaluation generally forms a part of the collection development policy of the library. Other reasons for
evaluation are:

- identification of collection adequacy including strengths and
  weaknesses;
- support for collection development policies;
- support for increased resources;
- accountability to parent institution.

It is from determining the quality, relevance, availability, accessibility and usage of collections that collection development policies
may be monitored and adjusted accordingly. By evaluating collections according to these criteria (bearing in mind that these are not
the only ones by any means) it is then possible to identify the
strengths and weaknesses and, where appropriate, to concentrate
resources on collection improvement or modification.

Through such evaluation methods collection development policies and other library procedures may be modified or even radically
altered. An imbalance between periodicals and monographs may
become apparent; large areas of 'dead' stock or gaps in certain subject areas may come to light; material may be taking too long to be
reshelved; turnaround time for material requested from other campuses or libraries may be too long; material may be deliberately
mis-shelved; material on closed shelves would perhaps be better
exploited on open access. Although information on the above issues

(and many more!) may become available, it would be naive to think that the resultant translation of this information into action, that is, the decision-making process, is based on rationality and a careful weighing of all the relevant factors. Further variables for inclusion are finance and other organizational factors, internal politics, personal ambitions, hidden agendas, innate conservatism, managerial competence etc.

Having identified collection weaknesses it may be necessary to use collection evaluation results to strengthen a request for extra resources. Although evidence per se is unlikely to guarantee a loosening of the institutional purse strings, professional judgement based on and supported by sound evidence will represent a minimum requirement. The other side of this coin is the accountability to the institutional management for the spending of either the current monies on collection development or the extra monies acquired through reasoned argument. Often such information will form part of regular reports or newsletters to library and academic staff and various committees representing the parent institution.

It is recognized that much has been written about collection evaluation and the variety of methods employed in the process. The intention here is not to provide comprehensive coverage of these evaluative exercises but to consider the more important and influential ones. A number of these topics overlap, for example document delivery services, accessibility and availability. The Further Reading section includes a number of important works in this area.

QUALITY AND RELEVANCE OF COLLECTIONS

This type of collection evaluation is based upon standards: through assessment by experts or through the use of bibliographies/citation analysis. Although the size of a collection may be an appropriate criterion for some institutions, it is not considered part of the quality/relevance criteria addressed in this section. Readers are referred to Lancaster (1993). Many of the quantitative approaches constitute a variation on the formula adopted by Clapp and Jordan (1965). This approach takes into account factors such as undergraduate student numbers and subjects, total student registrations and postgraduate fields offered. Such quantitative measures may be useful politically for upgrading services but may be of dubious value in judging the (in)adequacy of a collection for a specific body of users.

Expert Assessment

This method involves the direct evaluation of the collection by a person fully conversant with the literature of the subject area. This person who becomes the 'standard' may be a consultant or a group of specialists brought in from outside for this specific purpose or, indeed, a representative of the parent institution. Although assessment by experts may be an effective way of gaining impressionistic coverage of particular subject areas, it has certain inherent problems. First, the expert has to possess not only subject knowledge but also knowledge of the literature of that subject. Taking this one stage further, the expert has to be familiar not only with the nature of the courses studied at the institution but also the possibly heterogeneous nature of the students and their different needs. Second, if the subject experts are to be taken from the institution itself, it may be less than helpful to seek the views of people who may have been responsible for the development of the very collection under scrutiny. As is often the case when evaluating many areas in the social sciences, a variety of techniques may provide a more rounded picture of the service in question. The impressionistic approach described above could be a useful supporting methodology alongside more objective measures. There are few recent successful examples of the expert assessment approach (Burr, 1979).

Bibliographies/Citations

With this technique the collection is evaluated against a written standard – a subject bibliography, a list of periodicals or citations, the printed catalogue of a specialized library etc. – in order to determine what proportion is owned by the library. In some subject areas authoritative bibliographies or lists may be available for comparison although they may need updating or adjusting in some way (Elzy and Lancaster 1990). Where no such lists are available, it could be relatively straightforward to establish one using up-to-date texts (books or periodicals) and their references/bibliographies as the core sources on that subject.

An interesting approach to the use of citation analysis for evaluation was developed by Lopez (1983). This technique begins with the selection of a handful of highly relevant texts from each of which twenty references are chosen. Relevance is established by means of reviews and faculty interests. These titles are then checked against the collection. From those found further references are selected and the same process is repeated. This trawl through successive citations is continued up to four or five levels. The major problem of this technique lies in the possible bias if only the one library's contents are used to provide the references. For a more objective approach referred items should be acquired from other sources.

It should be remembered that the above evaluative methods treat the collections in the abstract and may bear little relation to usage. Use studies are considered later in this chapter. Less prevalent nowadays is the propensity for academic libraries to subscribe to particular research journals on the advice of validating or accrediting bodies. A combination of changes in validation procedures and financial constraints have encouraged many academic libraries to rationalize collections – and, in particular, journal subscriptions – and tailor them more tightly to the needs of the academic community.

AVAILABILITY

The previous section is concerned with establishing the quality and relevance of the library collection regardless of the immediate availability of specific items. Availability studies generally refer to the probability that items being sought in the library will be immediately available, that is, sitting on the shelves when the user requires them (Mansbridge, 1986).

Much small-scale research work was carried out during the 1970s and early 1980s on availability, particularly by Kantor (1976, 1978, 1981, 1984) and also by Whitlatch and Kieffer (1978) and Shaw (1980). In the last decade Revill (1987, 1988, 1991) has made regular contributions based on practical experience at Liverpool.

Some availability studies have been carried out by means of simulation, that is, by drawing a sample of items from the shelf list rather than from genuine user searches. A number of problems are inherent in this approach:

- it excludes items not acquired by the library
- it ignores the users' skills in retrieving items
- it fails to concentrate on 'live' items which are likely to be the biggest source of availability problems

The most widespread method of carrying out availability studies is through user surveys. On designated days or during specific periods of time library users are requested to complete availability slips to indicate their success in finding specific items in the library. Appendix III shows an example of this kind of slip. This slip is distributed to those entering or exiting the library and collected at a suitable point. The information taken from the completed slips will also indicate areas where the users failed to find certain items. Failure studies are considered below. Those who are searching for material in particular subject areas rather than specific items may be included in the survey since this will either result in a search for specific items (identified through the library catalogue) or from browsing the shelves (for which success rates may be entered on the survey slips).

Having collected a suitable number of item searches, the data are tabulated and analysed. From the previously mentioned research around 400 would seem to be the minimum sample required to generalize across the collection depending on its size. The materials availability rate is reached by dividing the number of successful searches by the total number of searches. Van House *et al.* (1990) and Kantor (1984) outline detailed procedures for carrying out such studies. The methods of Kantor allow the identification of the success of each stage of the search process rather than the final outcome as in the Van House procedure. The other side of this coin naturally is the failure rate and, particularly, the identification of reasons for failure to find the required material.

FAILURE STUDIES

While the above procedures identify success and failure, Urquhart and Schofield (1971) and Seymour and Schofield (1973) concentrated specifically on the reasons for user failure in the search process.

Items not acquired by the library

The library may have a policy of access (not necessarily immediately available) rather than collection-building. Non-acquisition may have resulted from lack of communication or misunderstanding about selection criteria between library and academic department. It may also reflect badly on the librarian's familiarity with the users' library needs. Alternatively it may be the result of financial constraints restricting book acquisitions or periodical subscriptions. A further explanation for failure at this stage may be that material has been ordered from the suppliers or is being prepared for circulation but has not yet appeared on the shelves. Most library catalogues would provide this information for users.

Possible remedies are:

1. Closer liaison between the library and academic departments;
2. Redeployment or extra staffing in technical service areas, for example ordering, material processing and cataloguing/acquisitions;
3. Questioning the efficiency of publishers, book suppliers and other agencies.

Items acquired but user unable to find on catalogue

Assuming the library catalogue contains the record being sought, there are a number of possible sources of failure. How familiar is the user with library catalogues and the specific catalogue being searched? Is it user friendly? Has the user received tuition in effective searching techniques? Are the catalogue entries intelligible, too detailed or confusing? Are cooperative cataloguing or downloaded records a help or a hindrance in this process? How determined or persistent is the user in searching the catalogue? Does the user have adequate and accurate information on the item being sought? Does the catalogue have enough access points and cross references to accommodate incomplete detail?

Possible remedies are:

1. Improved user education programmes, printed guides and worksheets, on- and off-screen help facilities including staff assistance;
2. Cataloguing policies consistent and helpful to the users.

Items located on catalogue but not on shelf

Having ascertained that the item should be located on the shelf, what is the probability that it will actually be there? If the item is not in use somewhere in the library, it should be on the shelf and available. As mentioned previously, its availability will depend very much on popularity, number of copies and length of loan period. Adding extra copies of popular material will undoubtedly improve availability as will a reduction in the loan period. A further problem associated with an item's disappearance is theft or deliberate mis-shelving. The current nature of further/higher education and library provision leads to greater competition among students for the collections of books and periodicals, partly through policies and partly through the erosion of libraries' purchasing power. A tiny minority of users will resort to theft or damaging items. The material being stolen or 'razored' tends to be those items in most demand by fellow students. A variety of security measures are in place in many institutions including security guards, CCTV and electronic tagging, but still the problem persists. Passing material to colleagues through windows is a current favourite in my own university.

The incidence of deliberate mis-shelving represents another anti-social activity which was highlighted recently at a British Psychological Society Conference in Plymouth (Brill, 1994). Survey research indicated that almost a quarter of the students questioned admitted hiding library books on different shelves to secure the book's availability (rather than through malice). This is difficult to counter other than through labour-intensive searching to identify misplaced items. Depending on the library's policy and staffing levels this may take days or weeks. Staffing levels are one determinant of the speed and efficiency of the library's reshelving operations. Any procedures which shorten the time during which an item is absent from its allotted place should be highlighted.

Many books and runs of periodicals have to be sent for binding during the year. In the past it was a fairly straightforward task to bind material at a less demanding time of year. This time is becoming increasingly difficult to find as usage of material becomes an all-year-round activity. Possible remedies are:

1. Closer liaison between library and departments to ensure adequate numbers of copies of material in demand, continuous monitoring of loan periods and identification of suitable periods for materials to be bound;
2. Appropriate security measures and continuing staff vigilance;
3. Deployment of staff in such a way that reshelving of material and 'tidying' the existing material is given a higher priority.

Items shelved appropriately but user unable to locate

A problem which some users experience, particularly if they are unfamiliar with the classification scheme in use, is that of wrongly transcribing the notation. In the Dewey decimal scheme, for example, the difference between 300.1, 301.01 and 301.1 may seem minor to an unfamiliar user but items located at these numbers may be physically some distance from each other. Similarly, users may not be totally familiar with various parallel or separate sequences – perhaps for large-size material, pamphlet items, official publications etc. – which have to be checked. It has to be said also that a number of libraries are woefully inadequate in terms of guiding and signposting. Other problems may be inadequate lighting, inappropriate shelving – too high or too low – or inadequate spine labelling.

Possible remedies are:

1. Improved user education programmes to explain important aspects of the classification scheme.
2. Phasing out of parallel/separate sequences where possible if they are problematic.
3. Improvement in guiding and signposting, a notorious hardy perennial of many library services. Although accompanied by resource implications, a lot could be learned from the retail service industries in this regard.
4. Adoption of a system of correcting or repairing spine labels as the material is circulated, where this is practicable.

As the above illustrates, a wealth of information can be provided through appropriate availability/failure studies which through their structured approach may shed light on many potential improvements in library service provision. Such information may not be brought to the attention of library managers other than through anecdotal evidence.

ACCESSIBILITY

A library no longer has to own all of the scholarly publishing output in a particular area if both bibliographic and physical access are possible electronically.

(Shapiro, 1992, p.50)

The context in which the terms access and accessibility are used has altered in recent years and, as a result, their meaning has become unclear. The access versus collection-building debate, already referred to, represents a good example of the waters being muddied. There is a simplistic assumption in some quarters that these policies are separate and discrete, whereas in reality most academic libraries will be providing a combination of both: collections of books, periodicals and other materials some of which may be available in electronic format or through interlibrary cooperation/loans, and access to electronic information through bibliographic and full-text databases, networks and electronic mail. The balance of provision will vary and will be dependent on library policies, their stage of development, institutional IT policies, financial constraints etc. The University of Aston (Corrall, 1993) and the University of Tilburg in Holland (Roes and Dijkstra, 1994) offer good examples of the possibilities of moving towards a more access-oriented and electronically based service.

As the quotation above implies, the concept of ownership and physical access to an item owned by a library is gradually being overshadowed by the provision of a route to an item regardless of its physical location. Elias (1992, p.4) has suggested that 'libraries will gain merit as a result of their connectivity rather than by their holdings'. It is also fair to stress the continuing importance placed by the academic community on the centrality of the 'owned collection' as support for the teaching and learning process.

Accessibility has been traditionally accepted as the time and effort expended by library clientele to reach the required item. In some respects this concept is intertwined with availability since some of the reasons for failing to retrieve an item may reside in 'barriers' inadvertently erected. However, there are two more fundamental ways in which accessibility to libraries themselves rather than individual items may be viewed:

Opening hours

Are the library's opening hours convenient for the majority of its clientele? Are certain areas restricted at certain times? Are users able to access telephone, other dial-up services and networks from outside? Are there special arrangements for non-traditional students, for example part-time students or distance learners?

Physical location

Does the library consist of one building, a number of branches, sites, campuses, departmental libraries etc.? How physically accessible are these buildings to the majority of users? Are they accessible to people with disabilities? Do users have to travel far? Is there a system of physical document delivery between service points? Is it effective? Does the interdisciplinary nature of many courses militate against the physical separation of libraries on subject grounds?

Inside the Library

To students and academic staff access to library services and facilities represents a factor which can produce feelings across a wide spectrum from satisfaction to high levels of frustration. The recent increases in student numbers that have not been matched by adequate resources have led to increased competition for not only library material but also tutors' time, student welfare and computing services, amongst other demands. For many less well resourced libraries such pressure has exacerbated access problems. At times the frustration factor can reach worrying proportions. What are some of the causes of this frustration?

- How easy is it to find an unoccupied OPAC terminal? Are there further OPACs on other floors? How much time and effort is involved in the search?
- How straightforward is translation from OPAC to shelf? Is the required item where it ought to be? (Problems of availability are discussed in the previous section.) Items can be available but inaccessible, for example in a relegated collection or store.
- How straightforward is it to reserve/recall requested items? Can it be carried out on the OPAC or is there a separate specific procedure?
- How straightforward is the process of ordering material which the library does not possess? Is there a system of quotas, limitations, charges, countersignatures etc before the interlibrary loan can be requested? How swift is the system in obtaining material from elsewhere? Are cooperative ventures more effective in supplying the required documents?
- Is there easy access to appropriate library staff? If a user requires assistance in finding material, is an enquiry or service point located nearby to provide help, either directional or subject specific?
- Do users have to queue for charging-out/returning/renewing books, registering with the library, using personal computers, microform reader/printers, audiovisual hardware, headphones, reprographic facilities etc.?
- Are users expected to book time for online searches, CD-ROM

stand-alone or networked systems, services to the blind/partially sighted, rooms for practising presentations or group discussions etc.?
- Do users have access to material in closed access areas? Is it immediate, within hours, days?

DOCUMENT DELIVERY

A number of the questions asked above relate to a library's ability to provide an efficient and speedy service by minimizing delays. The main areas are:

Requested items
These would include items owned by the library but currently on loan; items owned by one of the satellite/branch/departmental libraries; items located in an off-site store; items not owned by the library but borrowed from elsewhere.

Queuing
The extent of queuing represents an obvious parameter for judging the availability of a service whether it is supplying documents directly, supplying them indirectly via photocopying, CD-ROM networks or other databases, or provision of wider facilities.

Van House *et al.* (1990) offer straightforward advice on so-called 'requested materials delay'. They recommend for the particular service under consideration a system of logging the date of request and the date of arrival (or date on which notification is sent to the requester) with the delay measured in terms of hours, days, weeks etc. It is then the responsibility of the library to consider whether such delays fall within the targets set up or are acceptable within the library's policy guidelines. Improvements may need to be sought, for example streamlining or automation, more frequent deliveries, use of a 'fast lane' for urgent material, alternative cooperative arrangements etc.

Interlibrary Loans

Since the interlibrary loan service constitutes an increasingly important part of document delivery, it is worth considering its evaluation in a little more detail. The gradual shift of emphasis from teaching

to learning in most higher education institutions, with the concomi-
tant increase in information-handling skills programmes, financial
constraints and increasing dependency on CD-ROM and networking
facilities, have all placed enormous pressure on interlibrary loan
services. The result has been attempts by a number of libraries to
rationalize the service. These are some of the strategies adopted:

- placing limits on either particular groups of users, for example
  undergraduate/postgraduate/final year/academic staff, or on the
  number of requests per individual in a given period;
- charging for the requests to either the academic departments or
  the individual users (full cost or a proportion thereof);
- devolving interlibrary loan budgets to faculty/subject librarians
  to be committed using criteria negotiated between academic
  staff, library staff and users;
- vetting each request through faculty/subject librarians;
- receiving a realistic share of research funding made available to
  academic departments through research assessment exercises,
  other locally negotiated consultancies or other grants.

Many of the previously labour-intensive elements of the service
are nowadays being eliminated or curtailed through various automated means, for example integrated systems or e-mail. However,
the service is still very much one of administering and handling
materials for individual users.

The three major criteria for gauging the effectiveness of the interlibrary loan service are:

- success (or fill) rate – the relationship between the total number
  of requests and the number of requests successfully completed;
- turnaround time (or speed of supply or response time) – the
  amount of time elapsed between the initiation of a request and its
  completion;
- cost (or efficiency) – the level of resources consumed in the
  completion of interlibrary loan requests.

Examples taken from the literature covering success rate and turnaround time are publications by Willemse (1993) and Horton (1989).
Interlending as loss of investment is covered by Lowry (1990) and
for comparative purposes by MacDougall *et al.* (1990) and the
Centre for Interfirm Comparison (1984). Waldhart (1985) indicates
that success rates have improved over the last two decades (between
64% and 83% in the early 1970s to consistently over 75% more

recently). Information technology has been at the root of much of this improvement including the development of networks and union catalogues. The variables which affect the success rates include the difficulty of the requests themselves, the availability of reliable locational information, the accuracy of the requests and the perseverance of the borrowing library. Turnaround time includes these five stages:

- borrowing library processing time;
- request transit time;
- lending library processing time;
- material transit time;
- borrowing library processing time.

Library managers who wish to improve turnaround time will need to consider carefully each of these stages including the balance between automation and staffing, balance of staffing in interlibrary loan services and other departments, numbers of requests etc. No average turnaround times are provided since comparability involving so many variables would be fruitless. Each library must set, monitor and evaluate its own targets.

Costs of interlibrary loan services are subject to varying interpretations and the peculiarities of local circumstances and therefore few generalizations can be made from the literature. The difficulties involved in calculating costs include measurement of staff time and salaries for processes, automation costs and other administrative costs. Estimates of average costs and turnaround times are therefore only really of value to each individual library.

Electronic document delivery systems continue to develop with services such as CARL/Blackwell's UnCover which at a cost provides a fax of a document within 24 hours. Mitchell and Walters (1994), Rowley (1994) and Woodward (1994) provide details on the current state of play.

COLLECTION USAGE

One of the problems of measuring usage of library collections is the term 'use' itself. What does it mean?

1. A student borrows a library book for three weeks, does not open it and returns it.
2. A lecturer takes a reference book from the library shelf, copies down a statistic and leaves the building.

3. A student looks through a printed index to periodicals, finds a number of 'relevant' articles some of which turn out to be helpful, others not.

4. A student borrows half a dozen books, reads them thoroughly, writes an assignment demanding extensive reference to the books and receives a mark of 85%.

5. A student browses the shelves searching for books on a particular topic, finds a number of relevant titles, takes notes from some, photocopies from others and returns them to the shelves.

The above five situations demonstrate the difficulty of regarding 'use' as a catch-all word which encapsulates a measurable variable for subsequent analysis and interpretation. Unless specific methods are established to evaluate library collection usage (other than conventional circulation statistics), numbers 1 and 4 will be treated identically, numbers 2, 3 and 5 will be unrecorded.

It has to be accepted that to derive any meaningful interpretation of the benefits of library usage from evaluation, it is necessary to carry out some form of qualitative research, employing a range of methods including interview, questionnaire surveys, diaries etc. As with evaluation of user education and readers' enquiry services, the satisfaction survey is one method of gauging the benefits of a particular activity. These methods are covered in greater detail in Chapter 9.

Circulation Studies

The integrated systems which currently operate in many FE and HE libraries have the capacity – with varying degrees of sophistication – to provide statistics on borrowing library material. Such statistics may help in:

- indicating collection strengths and weaknesses;
- identifying items in heavy/little demand;
- measuring obsolescence;
- identifying usage in particular types of material, for example, audiovisual material, software, government publications, special collections or particular shelving locations;
- indicating which parts of the collection are borrowed by which user groups.

Analysis of circulation statistics in some studies (Kent, 1979;

Hardesty, 1981; Britten, 1990) have identified a number of trends, for example:

- As a rule of thumb the 80/20 rule (the Pareto effect) operates widely in terms of general usage patterns, that is, 80% of the usage seems to come from about 20% of the collection.
- Of those titles that circulate at all during a year, more than half circulate only once.
- 40% of the books added to stock in the study by Kent had not been borrowed in their first six years.
- 37% of items added to stock in the study by Hardesty had not been borrowed in their first five years.

For further details of the relative use of collections by means of circulation statistics readers should refer to Lancaster (1993).

Two other methods of evaluating collection usage are those described by Trueswell (1964, 1965, 1969) and Slote (1989). In the former the author has described a procedure for gauging what proportion of the collection accounts for what proportion of use, employing the last circulation date. In one academic library it was found that 40% of the collection would account for 99% of circulation. Slote's 'shelf time period' approach refers to the length of time a book sits on the shelf between circulations. Both approaches may be utilized to support the identification of obsolete or underused items for relegation, withdrawals etc.

In-house Usage

Circulation statistics represent only one part of total library collection usage and do not take into account material consulted within the confines of the library. Research results, although inconsistent and now rather outdated, suggest a correlation between borrowing books and in-house use (Hindle and Buckland, 1978; Lawrence and Oja, 1980), that is, material which circulates heavily is also consulted heavily on the premises. Such evaluation may also include periodical/journal usage. Indeed, in many academic libraries periodicals are not circulated outside the library and therefore a method of in-house usage evaluation is the only option. Methods adopted in such evaluation exercises are:

- tabulation of material not reshelved;
- observation of user behaviour;

- surveying users by placing questionnaires in selected materials and requesting their completion.

By far the most widely adopted method is to ask users not to reshelve items for a specific period and then library staff count the materials gathered for reshelving. The process may also be carried out at intervals during the day, on particular days of the week or particular weeks of the term to determine periods of heaviest or least use. It would seem sensible that such evaluative exercises be carried out for specific purposes at specific points in time since they are by their nature staff-intensive.

Periodical usage may be measured by stapling a slip of paper on the cover of unbound issues (and sticking slips on the front of bound volumes) and requesting users to indicate their usage by signing or ticking. A similar approach may be followed when evaluating the use of reference material – having a slip of paper prominently displayed inside the book on which the type of use or user may be easily identified.

Benefits of Book and Periodical Usage

In order to gain qualitative information from library clientele about their usage and activities within the library, surveying would be the most effective method. This method is similar to those used in failure studies or user education evaluation. In this way information may be gleaned on students' use of material, time spent reading/studying, their subject areas or departmental affiliations, status etc. Hamburg *et al.* (1974) adopted the idea of taking the reader's time exposed to the material as an indicator of usage. This was an attempt to develop a more sensitive measure which focused on the user. Such information was meant to provide a more accurate picture. Library users may also be interviewed as they are working or after they have finished. This process may be structured in terms of areas of the library, seating patterns, time slots etc. User studies and surveys are covered in Chapter 9.

FURTHER READING

Buckland, M. K. (1975) *Book Availability and the Library User*. New York: Pergamon Press.

Ford, G. (1990) *Review of Methods Employed in Determining the Use of Library Stock*. (BNBRF Report 43). London: BNBRF.

Gorman, G. E. and Howes, B. R. (1989) *Collection Development for Libraries*. London: Bowker-Saur.

Lancaster, F. W. (1982) 'Evaluating collections by their use.' *Collection Management* **4**, 15–43.

Mansbridge, J. (1986) 'Availability studies in libraries.' *Library and Information Science Research* **8**(4), 299–314.

Nisonger, T. E. (1992) *Collection Evaluation in Academic Libraries: a Literature Guide and Annotated Bibliography*. Englewood, Colo.: Libraries Unlimited.

Waldhart, T. J. (1985) 'Performance evaluation of interlibrary loan in the United States: a review of research.' *Library and Information Science Research* **7**, 313–331.

Winkworth, I. (1991) 'Performance measures and performance indicators.' In Jenkins, C. and Morley, M. (eds.). *Collection Management in Academic Libraries*. Aldershot: Gower. pp.57–93.

CHAPTER SIX

User education

It is imperative that every library develop and engage in a
planned, and preferably assessable, programme of user education
in close cooperation with subject teachers.

(Library Association, 1982, p.27)

The issues covered in this chapter are:

- a brief history of user education evaluation;
- the purpose of user education evaluation;
- the focus of user education evaluation;
- the methods of user education evaluation.

Throughout the last twenty five years a number of terms have
been in vogue to characterize user education. This latter term is generally favoured in the UK, whilst in US academic libraries
'bibliographic instruction' has been the preferred term. More
recently 'information-handling skills' has gained popularity, perhaps reflecting the current emphasis on electronic information
sources in preference to the conventional book-based concept. Some
writers have attempted to disaggregate the processes involved in
library orientation and those in bibliographic instruction, and this is
the convention followed in this chapter.

Library orientation which sometimes forms part of a larger programme of user education requires a different set of objectives to
those in more formal teaching sessions. Whilst the majority of UK
academic libraries undertake library orientation sessions – either
stand-alone or as part of larger programmes – the picture for other user
education activity is more patchy, with different practices in different
libraries (Cowley and Hammond 1987). For up-to-date coverage of
the state of user education the reader is referred to Fleming (1990).

Since these formal user education sessions represent educational programmes, their evaluation poses many of the problems inherent in other 'learning experiences' in which the students participate, for example:

- Which parts of the programme content should be evaluated?
- How should the learning outcomes be evaluated?
- How should the teacher, teaching methods and learning environment be evaluated?
- Should student attitudes be evaluated and, if so, how?
- Is there a place for independent observers?
- What action should be taken to improve the programme (where necessary)?

One major difference between library programmes and other educational programmes is that the former will be delivered by subject/learning resources librarians (nomenclature varies) who will normally have precious little time – and often this will have been grudgingly given or hard fought – in which to achieve their objectives. Invariably other educational programmes will range over a number of weeks, months or over a whole semester or year. Librarians are therefore generally under pressure to 'make an impact' since either they may not get a second chance to develop or reinforce a programme or, as in the case illustrated in Figure 6.1, the length of time between elements of a programme can be depressingly long. This time factor goes some way to explaining the reasons for the reluctance of many academic libraries to evaluate their user education programmes (Morgan 1992). This survey of higher education libraries showed that over half of the libraries did not evaluate their programmes. The main reason given was insufficient time.

The forms which user education programmes take may be many and varied. Teaching sessions may be:

- single or a series spread over a long period;
- timetabled and/or integrated into the course structure or arranged on a 'need to know' basis;
- lectures, seminars, workshops, demonstrations etc.;
- delivered via one instructional method or a combination, perhaps incorporating workbooks, slides, videos, interactive IT facilities with supporting flipcharts, overhead transparencies, examples etc.

These elements are by no means exhaustive but merely illustrative

of the range of types of user education sessions which are currently
in use and therefore open to evaluation.

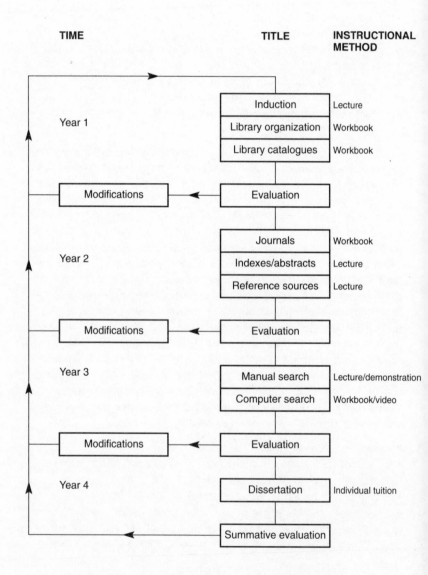

Figure 6.1. An example BEd user education programme.

EVALUATION: A BRIEF HISTORY

User education had its heyday in the 1970s both in the UK and the US in that the literature was replete with much theoretical under-pinning and comparisons of teaching and learning methods (Lockwood, 1979; Hardesty *et al.* 1986). Very few evaluative exer-cises were carried out because in many quarters user education was considered to be a 'good thing' and consequently did not require evaluation. Benson (1980, p.53) has expressed these feelings admirably:

Bibliographic instruction seems to be perceived by many librarians simply as a self-evident social good, not needing an extensive rationale or empiri-cal evidence to substantiate its effectiveness or even to support the need for it. Much of the literature of bibliographic instruction resembles a dialectic with the antithesis missing.

Nevertheless, some valuable projects were carried out, particu-larly in the US – those of Hardesty *et al.* (1979), Lubans' collection (1978) and Werking (1980) are examples. The study by Fjallbrant (1977) is one of the foremost of the European examples. Throughout the 1980s the New Right's preoccupation with efficiency within the public services sector considered in Chapter 1 should have signalled a similar strive within academic libraries to evaluate user education programmes. The literature, however, did not show such a move although there were some notable exceptions which described actual evaluations and results, for example Hatchard and Toy (1984) and Tiefel (1989). More recently, the emphasis has swung back to evalu-ation of different instructional methods such as Edwards (1991), Carpmael *et al.* (1991), Lawson (1989) and Bluck *et al.* (1994) in the search for variety and more effective methods.

WHY EVALUATE USER EDUCATION?

There are a handful of reasons for wanting to evaluate a user educa-tion programme, any of which may pertain to a particular library. First, and the paramount reason for many, will be improvement of the programme itself. Evaluation carried out while the programme is running, known as formative evaluation, will often iron out prob-lems which the presenter of the session may have overlooked or failed to address at the planning stage. It therefore has a diagnostic function. Such improvements could range from the easily rectifiable (the overhead projector obscuring some participants' view of the screen) to the less easily rectifiable (the conceptual content of a literature searching session being pitched at too high/low a level). Very often the programme developer does not have time for a sophisticated statistical analysis. Therefore formative evaluation may consist of simplified versions of questionnaires or tests used for the summative evaluation at the end of the programme. These latter reports can prove beneficial to the library or institution managers so that policy decisions on benefits and costs of such programmes may be made with some confidence. For further elaboration of formative/summative approaches the reader should refer to Scriven (1967).

Whilst the librarian may be tempted to alter the programme following evaluation, it would be wise to reflect on it and consider whether improvements are necessary. Certain evaluation techniques, particularly the more subjective approaches where respondents complete a brief questionnaire following a teaching session, need to be treated with care and scepticism to ensure that hastily made modifications are not carried out unnecessarily. It is hoped that such improvements will help to make the students more effective library and information users, an objective which will also be evaluated via assignments, observations etc. This leads on to the second reason for evaluation.

Discovering how far the aims and objectives of the programme have been met is of vital importance. Some of the objectives may be short term and easily evaluated whilst some may be long term and more difficult. It may be possible to explore – either formally or informally – whether students' attitudes towards the library or particular aspects of it have changed at all. A more difficult task will be to gauge whether the transferable skills are being transferred.

Third, evaluation may be a requirement of the library's management, the parent institution's administration or the relevant faculties/departments. Any of these stakeholders may feel that the subject librarians have to demonstrate accountability in this way, and evaluation – perhaps with a view to exploring cost-effectiveness – may help to serve that purpose. It may be the case that the library's management or faculty needs to compare different instructional methods. It may also be the case that the institutional political system requires that user education programmes are justified in terms of bidding for extra resources or in terms of 'visibility'. In order to argue successfully for extra resources, user education programmes may have to be seen as efficient and effective. Indeed it may be felt in some universities that the academic-related salary scales of subject/faculty librarians need to be justified by means of evaluation. Some have suggested rather cynically that the evaluation of user education constitutes a method of trying to increase the status of academic librarians in the eyes of the faculties and should be carried out by academic staff (Lester, 1979; Line, 1983).

A fourth reason posited by Fleming (1990), which is already happening at some universities and is visible on the horizon at others, is for the results of student evaluation of user education to be incorporated into staff appraisal systems. Similar feedback following the normal course monitoring and evaluation may currently be taken into account in academic staff appraisal procedures. Such information would feed into the appraisal system along with information from other sources, for example from the faculties, peer groups and line managers, to form a holistic view. This is considered further in Chapter 8.

DISADVANTAGES OF EVALUATION

There are two major disadvantages of evaluating user education which are more widely applicable to other areas within performance assessment: lack of time and lack of expertise.

Lack of Time

Any kind of evaluation, if carried out properly, is time consuming. As previously mentioned, the time that librarians require to deliver effective user education programmes is sometimes severely constrained and therefore even more precious. The temptation may be overwhelming to fill all the available time with teaching. The importance of evaluation is such that, wherever possible, time should be found for it. Some institutions, particularly in the US, have established library research offices whose staff are employed specifically to carry out operational research including the evaluation of information-handling skills programmes. By making such a move, either evaluation may be carried out where it has not been done in the past or librarians may concentrate on delivering the programmes in the knowledge that they are being properly evaluated. In the UK the closest the universities get to a similar scenario is where librarianship courses are taught. In these institutions, very often as an integral element of student project, dissertation or higher degree work, small-scale research provides an appropriate opportunity for such evaluation.

Lack of Expertise

In the past the skills and techniques which are the requirements of librarians involved in evaluation have been learned when the need has arisen. Often the skills acquired as part of librarianship training have to be modified or 'topped up' when faced with the situation of needing to evaluate a user education programme. Nowadays more emphasis is placed on research methods including surveys and tests. However, librarians have been reluctant to seek advice from and draw on the expertise of other departments within institutions, for example education, statistics or social sciences, opening themselves up to the accusation of being isolationist in evaluation matters. In fact, this was one of the suggested improvements to come out of the surveys described in Chapter 4. It is in the interests of the departments to participate in this process since one of the major aims of user education is to improve the product of student endeavours – assignments, bibliographies etc. – and in the longer term, to apply these transferable information-handling skills in the wider context of the world of work.

WHAT TO EVALUATE?

The best way to illustrate what has to be evaluated is by means of a suitable scenario. 'How to evaluate', although briefly alluded to, will be explored further in the next section. Figure 6.2 shows the framework on which the scenario will hang.

Scenario

The BA Information Systems and Social Science is a newly validated three-year undergraduate programme which attempts to integrate two fields of study to produce a vocational qualification, underpinned by concepts and research methods taken from the social sciences. To help in the harmonization of the disciplines within the degree and as an important part of the final assessment, students are required to undertake a 15 000 word dissertation.

To provide library and information support for this project, the

Time	Activity	Method
9.00 – 9.30	Aims and objectives	Talk, exercise
9.30 – 10.00	Introduction to the literature	Talk
10.00 – 10.30	Defining research proposal	Exercise
10.30 – 11.00	Coffee	
11.00 – 11.30	Search methods	Video
11.30 – 1.00	Sources: printed and electronic	Discussion, demonstration, exercises
1.00 – 2.00	Lunch	
2.00 – 2.30	Feedback from exercises	Discussion
2.30 – 3.00	Citing references etc.	Talk, exercise
3.00 – 3.15	Tea	
3.15 – 3.45	Interlibrary loans and other document delivery	Talk, demonstration
3.45 – 4.30	What is expected? Examples of past dissertations	Discussion
4.30 – 5.00	Review and evaluation	Discussion

Figure 6.2. Searching the literature: a scenario.

two subject librarians (the one covers computing and information systems, the other covers the social sciences) have built into the course a one-day workshop called 'Searching the literature'. This programme is based on the aims and objectives agreed between subject librarians (who formed part of the course planning group) and relevant academic staff. Since there are thirty final year students the workshop is repeated three times, the teaching being shared between academic and library staff. The format is shown in Figure 6.2.

In the short term the extent to which the aims and objectives of the workshops have been met is gauged by means of the following:

1. results of the exercises;
2. evaluation questionnaires;
3. review discussion;
4. observations of academic staff;
5. observations of library staff.

In the longer term the evaluation needs to take into account the quality of the final product – the dissertation. Although direct causal links may be difficult to assign, the students' skills and techniques in making more judicious and sophisticated use of the library and information systems available should be reflected in the final product. At this point discussions between tutors and librarians and also between students and librarians may be a fruitful method of gauging the effectiveness of the library support services and also the attitudes of the students towards the library.

Using the illustration of the scenario and the simple model outlined in Figure 6.3, the following are some of the issues that may need to be addressed when evaluating such a programme, categorized into process, content and product. In the model the input consists mainly of resources (staff time, teaching rooms, finance etc).

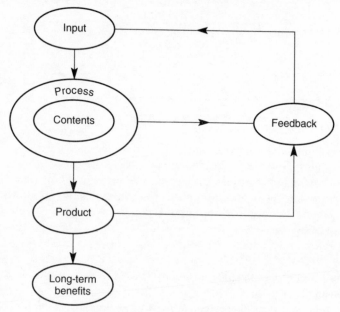

Figure 6.3. User education: a systems model.

Process

- Was the room adequate in size, layout etc.?
- Was the programme too long/short/unbalanced?
- Did most students participate when required?
- Was ten the right group size for such a workshop?
- Was joint teaching appropriate for this programme?
- Were presentation styles appropriate?
- Were the teaching aids helpful?
- Did the students have adequate opportunity to ask questions?
- Was the timing of the workshops right?

Content

- Was all the content necessary?
- How much of the content was new to the students?
- Was the content pitched at the appropriate intellectual level?
- Was coverage comprehensive or were there some gaps?
- Did students perceive the value of the contents?
- Did the exercises reinforce the content?
- Was the supporting literature helpful?
- Was the material suitably paced throughout the day?
- Did the material build upon knowledge/skills already gained?

Product

Cognitive Objectives

- Did the students acquire the knowledge?

For example, did the students understand the structure of the literature? Did they know which sources were likely to be of most help when searching for particular topics? Were concepts such as Boolean logic, proximity operators etc. clear to them?

Psychomotor Objectives

- Did the students acquire certain skills?

For example, did the students acquire the skills to get into the network and search the CD-ROM databases? Were the students able to read from and take photocopies of journal and other material using microfilm and microfiche facilities?

Affective Objectives

● Did the students acquire the right attitudes?

For example, did the students develop a positive attitude towards the library? Did some students still feel apprehension about tackling library and information-based problems? Did students have the confidence to try certain equipment, services and facilities without 'appearing foolish'?

It is hoped that most of these questions are answered by means of the short-term evaluation methods 1–5 listed above, with a combination of participants' perceptions/reactions, workshop results and student project achievement.

HOW TO EVALUATE?

The variables which constitute the 'how' of evaluating user education programmes are many, for example:

● subjective and objective approaches;
● a variety of methods including testing, surveying (interviews, written questionnaires etc.), observing, illuminative evaluation etc.;
● different evaluative perspectives including those of students, library instructors, library managers, academic staff, independent observers and others;
● process-orientated and product-orientated methods;
● formal and informal evaluation procedures.

It is important to remember that the evaluation methods used depend on the purpose of that evaluation and the available resources. It is axiomatic that no one single method will provide the complete evaluative picture. The more and varied are the methods, the greater the likelihood of acquiring accurate and holistic feedback on the user education programme. Such a set of methods will produce a 'triangulation' effect – the same question being answered in different ways (see also the section Illuminative Evaluation).

In order to disaggregate some of the variables referred to above, it may be helpful to consider the main evaluative methods which are utilized in user education programmes. The two main categories are surveys and tests. These and other research methodologies are explored in greater detail in Chapter 9 for use in other evaluative contexts.

ASSESSMENT METHODS

Surveys

For the purposes of this section a survey represents a whole range of methods including questionnaires, discussion groups and interviews. These methods tend to create a large amount of qualitative material that reflects the perceptions of the participants – students, library instructors, academic staff and others (Frick, 1990). They are therefore largely subjective approaches – either formal or informal – which concentrate more on the process of the programme rather than on the product.

Questionnaires

The questionnaire has been, and still is, the most commonly found method of evaluating user education programmes (Morgan, 1990). The main reasons for this are: its comparative ease of completion; the potentially good response rate if administered at the teaching session; the librarian's presence often enabling clarification of problematic questions; and anonymity leading to more honest responses. Some of the disadvantages of the questionnaire are: requirement for an immediate response without adequate time for reflection; necessarily subjective approach; difficulty in designing a 'foolproof' questionnaire; difficulty in measuring attitudes; possible lack of rigour. The same pros and cons apply whether the questionnaire is administered to staff, students or any other participants.

Participants must be aware of the programme's aims and objectives so that they may be able to judge their progress in achieving them. There is a danger that participants may make a judgement on objectives which they themselves have set and which may be at odds with those set by the organizers/instructors. Equally, evaluation should be carried out not only through the objectives model, since unintended benefits may result from the programme. Such views would normally be made clear in follow-up sessions which need to be open- ended to take account of these benefits apparent to the students, although not anticipated by the organizers.

Discussion groups

Discussing the effectiveness of a user education programme with participants can be productive in terms of formative and/or summative evaluation. Depending on the timing of such follow-up events, it is probable that an immediate reaction to the programme or part of the programme would be given, with neither adequate time for reflection nor a realistic projection of possible long-term benefits. Discussion (or feedback) groups should ideally be integrated into the user education programme and timetabled accordingly. So that the group's discussion may gather fruitful responses that can be fed back into improving the programme, it is vital that the discussion leader/facilitator has the appropriate skills and personality. This person (or indeed several individuals drawn from the library and academic staff) should have the skills necessary to draw out problems, themes, constructive criticism, to generalize from individual difficulty where appropriate, and to conduct proceedings in an open and non-threatening environment where all participants are trusting of each other. The discussion may also benefit from the adoption of a semi-structured questionnaire which the facilitator uses as a means of guidance to steer the discussion when necessary.

It may be appropriate for the discussion group to be facilitated by academic staff or an independent evaluator without the library staff present. Such a process may provide a more open discussion where participants feel more free to express their opinions. As long as the responses are fed back to library staff, this could be a productive way forward.

One of the problems encountered with discussion groups involves the recording of the significant issues which have been raised. The proceedings may be tape recorded although this may inhibit participation particularly in the early stages, or someone may take notes to highlight the major themes. Nichols (1993) and Freedman and Bantly (1986) provide examples of cases where feedback groups were used effectively for evaluation purposes.

A more unstructured approach involving groups consists of eliciting impressionistic views of a programme at the end of a session. Alongside other methods, this may help to build up a clearer overall picture.

Interviews
Although labour intensive the one-to-one interview can be an effective method of drawing out individuals' opinions and knowledge acquired, particularly since some students are apprehensive about speaking up in group or seminar situations (Patton, 1990). For the sake of consistency and ease of collation and analysis, the interviewer normally makes use of a checklist. In this way all the desired

areas of discussion are covered whilst still allowing for the exploration of unplanned routes. The success of this method depends on the questions being asked, the skills of the interviewer, the openness and honesty of the respondents, the recording and analysis of the information and the improvement of the programme where necessary.

Due to the time-consuming nature of the exercise a more sensible approach may be to interview a representative sample of participants rather than the whole group, which would be the ideal. The problems of choosing representative samples, interpretation of questions and accuracy of responses are addressed in Chapter 9.

Tests

The method which is most criticized and which has been paradoxically that most commonly reported in the literature is the written test. Its use has been most widespread in the US where tests such as the Feagley Test (Feagley, 1955; Perkins, 1965) had a significant influence in the 1960s and 1970s, although less in recent years. The way that the written test has been described – the 'agricultural-botany paradigm' – and subsequently put into practice (Hardesty et al., 1979) represents a good model for those wishing to emulate this method. Parlett and Hamilton (1976, p.85) describe the method in agricultural terms:

Students – rather like plant crops – are given pretests (the seedlings are weighed and measured) and then submitted to different experiences (treatment conditions). Subsequently, after a period of time, their attainment (growth or yield) is measured to indicate the relative deficiency of the methods (fertilizers) used.

In this model the students are given a test to evaluate their current skills level. They then attend a user education session or programme to try to improve on this level. Finally, they are tested to evaluate how much improvement has taken place. Alternatively, a control group may be used so that a comparison may be made following the library programme. Such an example is provided by Dykeman and King (1983). This latter method also helps to eliminate the possibility of bias in the questions.

While tests per se are relatively easily administered, they may only measure short-term retention of skills and knowledge which students may then fail to apply in different information-seeking situations, that is, the skills have not been transferred. Those who are in favour of applying the 'hard' research methods – accounts of which often reach the journal literature mainly because of their measurability – need to take into account the other variables which impact upon a user education programme and its individual participants. Such variables include the learning environment (the library, relations with faculty, study facilities), individual situations in relation to course workload, personal motivation and perceptions about the worth of such a programme to the students' own goals. The applicability of these methods when trying to justify user education programmes to parent institutions must be considered with some caution. Kaplowitz (1986) and Tiefel (1989) provide examples good example of pre- and post-testing.

Tests – using the term in a more informal sense – can also be appropriate in examining whether students have applied the knowledge and skills acquired in user education programmes in their academic course or assignment work. This may be done either through specific library exercises or through cooperation with academic staff in marking (Hanson, 1984; Feinberg and King, 1992).

Other Evaluation Methods

Illuminative Evaluation

This phrase coined by Trow (1977) represents a research strategy rather than a standard methodological package. This strategy, which has been adopted successfully to evaluate innovative projects, deemphasizes the initial aims and objectives of the programme, stressing the production of insights rather than testing hypotheses. The normal process of illuminative evaluation includes more than one method although the decision on which methods are appropriate is made on an individual basis. The methods usually include subjective ones, for example participant observation, semistructured interviews. Results of student achievement tests can also be incorporated into the data collection process. The advantage of this strategy is its multidimensional nature, the plurality of methods providing a fuller picture. The disadvantages are that the method lacks objectivity and can be very time consuming and labour intensive. Examples of this approach have been provided by Harris (1977) and De Silva (1985).

Observation

In terms of evaluation, observation may be applied in two specific ways. First, there is observation of those participating in the user education programme itself by peers, independent observers or academic staff in the same way as those training to become teachers would be observed as part of their teaching practice. Responses are then fed back to the programme's organizers/deliverers in order to improve it. Second, in order to judge the effects of the user education programme, actual use of the library and its facilities by students may be observed rather than relying on the students' own perceptions of how it was used. Observing the processes that students go through when carrying out library exercises following a user education session could be informative.

LONG-TERM BENEFITS

Much user education involves the acquisition and deployment of information-handling skills which can be transferred into other situations either outside the immediate learning environment or after the student has left the course. In the 1990s there is much emphasis in education on transferable skills. Gauging the long-term effectiveness of courses which purport to teach transferable skills is therefore important but fraught with difficulties. Follow-up questionnaires can be used so that students' perceptions of, for example, user education courses, library service uptake and use of specific facilities, may be monitored. Response rates for such exercises are usually very low. Such programmes have to rely on users' views of how they searched the library differently or how their attitudes and learning habits changed. 'Hard' evidence of long-term benefits derived from user education are difficult to come by (Selegean, et al., 1983), but research does indicate that a variety of methodologies – particularly a combination of quantitative and qualitative – provides the fullest and most accurate reflection of effectiveness.

FURTHER READING

Much of the empirical work in user education evaluation was carried out during the 1970s and early 1980s. Recent evaluation projects are few and far between in the literature; however the following give helpful overviews. Association of College and Research Libraries (1983) *Evaluating*

Bibliographic Instruction: a Handbook. Chicago: American Library Association

Cowley, J. (1988) *A Survey of Information Skills Teaching in UK Higher Education* (British Library Research Paper No.47). London: British Library.

Dolphin, P. (1990) 'Evaluation of user education programmes.' In Fleming, H. (ed.). *User Education in Academic Libraries.* London: LA Publishing, pp.73–89.

Fjallbrant, N. and Malley, I. (1984) *User Education in Libraries* (2nd ed.). London: Clive Bingley.

Fleming, H. (1986) 'User education in academic libraries in the UK.' *British Journal of Academic Librarianship* 1(1), 18–40.

Gibson, C. (1992) 'Accountability for bibliographic instruction programs in academic libraries: key issues for the 1990s.' *Reference Librarian* 38, 99–108.

Tiefel, V. (1989) 'Evaluating a library user education programme: a decade of experience.' *College and Research Libraries* 50(2), 248–259.

CHAPTER SEVEN

Readers' enquiry services

> If the doctor, surgeon or lawyer were to work at the level of accuracy suggested, there would be an outcry, as 45% of their clients were wrongly diagnosed, died on the operating table or were unjustly incarcerated.
>
> (Burton 1990, p.211)

The issues addressed in this chapter are:

- reasons for evaluating readers' enquiries;
- the elements to be evaluated;
- the methods of evaluating.

In recent times it has become increasingly difficult to provide an efficient and effective service to library clientele. The enormous increases in the recruitment of students which the university and FE sectors have seen recently have placed heavy burdens on library staff already committed to developments in computer-based services, modularization, student-centred and resource-based learning and a variety of modes of course delivery, to name but some. As part of the library's customer-oriented service the work carried out at the enquiry desk represents a significant contribution to helping users on an individual basis. This particular service taken alongside its other conventional partners, for example circulation of materials, user education programmes, current awareness and bulletin services, goes some way to plugging the information gaps inevitably left by the other services.

The nature of enquiry work makes demands, amongst other things, on one precious commodity – the librarian's time. This labour-intensive service is often perceived – by academic and library staff – as the major interface between user and library, other than the issue of books. The service therefore needs to be evaluated in the same way as the other elements of the library jigsaw in order to gauge its success in helping to meet the information needs of users.

READERS' ENQUIRIES

The terminology which surrounds this type of work is varied. Readers' enquiries, user services, customer information desk, enquiry service point, reference and information service, information desk, 'knocking on the librarian's door' – these and others refer to a face-to-face enquiry in which clients require a service over and above the use of the library for studying or for the issue/return of books. These 'information transactions' may take place in different locations, for example:

- at the issue/circulation desk (which may double as an enquiry desk in a small campus library);
- at the designated information service point;
- at the subject enquiry desk (which may be separate from the information service point and will probably be staffed by academic librarians with particular subject expertise);
- in the librarian's office (in many libraries these encounters are positively encouraged and greatly appreciated; indeed in some libraries, as in other professions, regular surgeries are held).

The service may be provided at a combination of these locations and may involve more than one librarian. At some service points the presence of more than one librarian would be highly desirable – at peak times positively essential – to cope with the enquiry flow when a colleague is called away on an enquiry.

To say that the range of enquiries received is broad is an understatement. The librarian is expected to satisfy the whole range – from the simplest directional request to the supplying of information based on a bibliographical search of international electronic databases. The latter will of course take a little longer! The more protracted enquiry may be postponed or referred to another colleague or agency, although a start may be made on it at the enquiry point. A system that appears to be effective in a number of academic libraries involves the provision of an initial service point to act as an 'information filter' or gateway. The librarian at this point would perhaps require skills different from those of the librarians working at the subject enquiry points. Many of the simple directional requests can be filtered out at this stage and the more complex subject enquiries referred, as appropriate, to other service points or colleagues.

How individual library staff carry out their duties is dependent upon the prevailing service ethos, the modus operandi of the librarian and the nature of the enquiry. Staff will either *assist* users to locate specific information through guidance and facilitation and/ or staff will *instruct* users in how to search (through individual tuition where appropriate) or refer them to another agency or librarian. In reality the outcomes will be reached through a combination of these activities with the boundaries very often blurred. Such steps would be taken in the knowledge that time spent on individuals may have to be minimized for the sake of helping a larger number of people.

In many libraries nowadays the readers' enquiry service performs a more intensive function than previously was the case. Greater demands are being made on the service throughout the full period of library opening hours. Students have been – and still are being – encouraged to take more responsibility for their own learning and many have become less dependent on tutors and academic staff. This philosophy, driven by pragmatic and logistical as well as for sound educational reasons, inevitably sends in the library's direction greater numbers of students some of whom will have yet to acquire (and may never do so!) the necessary information-handling skills with which to do justice to the library's potential. Although user education programmes strive to support students in their independent endeavours, readers' enquiries and one-to-one library tutorials form an essential point of need service.

WHY EVALUATE READERS' ENQUIRY SERVICES?

Some of the reasons for assessing performance at the enquiry interface mirror those for assessing other services including book and periodical collections, user education and interlibrary loan services. They are accountability, productivity and measurability. A readers' enquiry service forms an essential part of an increasingly complex organization and therefore a realistic evaluation – preferably by means of quantitative and qualitative methods – is necessary to gain an overview. The management culture of some academic libraries indicates that monitoring and evaluating of enquiry services form an integral and taken-for-granted part of wider evaluative processes. However, a recent survey (Morgan, 1993) indicated that three out of four UK HE libraries carry out no evaluation of their enquiry services. Quantitative details have been collected under the COPOL/SCONUL umbrella (SCONUL, 1992) for a number of years but with less emphasis on effectiveness.

Many other assessment processes, for example staff appraisal, may become culturally acceptable rather than being viewed as isolated events which raise eyebrows. However, before this happens, procedures need to be generally agreed, carried out successfully a number of times and be perceived as fair and equitable.

The productivity and measurability briefly referred to above, whilst they may represent examples of the new managerialist penchant for quantifying everything, may also provide evidence – both quantitative but more importantly qualitative – to support the negotiation for increases in resources. Nowadays, solid evidence is an absolute minimum for justifying a service to the parent institution or other fund providers, especially when the service is so heavily reliant on the skills and professional expertise of the library staff paid for out of the resource-draining staffing budget.

Enquiry and reference services are often perceived as adjuncts to the user education programmes. Some have argued in the past (Lester, 1979) that enquiry and reference services are what librarians do best rather than the attempts to reach the mass of the student body through user education programmes using skills which may be alien to some academic librarians. More accurately the answer may lie somewhere between the two. They are complementary activities with a symbiotic relationship. Those who have experienced clearly structured and enlightening user education programmes often come away enthused and highly motivated about the information world and ask questions at enquiry points prompted directly by the programmes delivered. Similarly, those who have missed out on such sessions will often prompt the librarians to organize programmes or sessions to fill a gap. Although this scenario is rather simplistically drawn, the close connection between and the complementarity of the two activities is fairly clear. The rationale for evaluating the effectiveness of enquiry work is no less strong than that for user education. Could it be the case that the effectiveness of user education is perceived to be easier to gauge than that of readers' enquiry services?

WHAT TO EVALUATE?

Readers' enquiry work comprises a complex set of variables any or all of which may be relevant for the purposes of evaluation. In exploring the nature of an enquiry and therefore its potential evaluation, there are a number of stages through which the process may develop. Here is an example of such a process:

1. The student perceives a library/information-related problem
Does the user attempt to find a solution without approaching the enquiry desk perhaps through apprehension or embarrassment? Does the user approach the desk? Davinson (1980) makes a point about the importance of spatial considerations in interpersonal communications which is particularly pertinent to the reference interview.

2. If the user decides to approach the enquiry desk/librarian in office, he or she needs to formulate the problem into words to explain it clearly to the library staff
Is there a librarian waiting for the approach? Does the librarian convey an attitude and manner that encourage the user to seek assistance? Does the librarian put the user at ease immediately? Are invisible barriers put in place? Body language can play a significant part in the interview process, particularly in the early (possibly uncertain) stage. This stage is crucial since some users would rather their questions went unanswered than approach the forbidding figure at the desk and reveal their ignorance. The librarian now becomes directly involved in the interviewing process and starts to negotiate, where necessary, in order to move towards a solution.

3. Discussion takes place to clarify the requirements of the user
Is the user asking the right questions? For example 'Could you tell me where the books on racism are?' The student is in reality looking for recent writings (journal or newspaper articles?) on racism in the workplace. The specific requirements are gleaned only through coaxing, 'teasing out the information' and negotiation. Is the level, format, language, currency of the required information clear to the librarian? Is there instruction involved in the encounter or is it purely fact-finding? Is the subject too obscure or complex to answer? How interested is the librarian in the problem? Should it be referred to a colleague or another agency? If so, is the enquirer happy with that? Is there a rapport between enquirer and librarian? Is referral a sign of

the librarian's professional inadequacy or professionalism?

4. The user is either provided with a solution or is assisted in finding a solution or instructed in the use of a bibliographical tool etc. Does the user understand any tuition provided? If facts are given, are they the required ones, at an appropriate level, in sufficient quantity and quality, in a suitable format etc.? Has it taken too long to reach the answer? Did the librarian exercise the appropriate skills in finding the answer? Were a number of different sources used or just one? Were IT services/facilities necessary? Was the location (enquiry desk/other service point/librarian's office) conducive to the interview? Was there excessive noise, interruption, heat, adequate lighting, a queue, ringing telephones or any other environmental factors which may have adversely affected the user and librarian? Was the user genuinely satisfied with the outcome?

The four main ingredients of these stages which encapsulate the enquiry interview are: factual answers; negotiating skills (librarian/user); attitudes (librarian/user); and provision of instruction. These are the major elements in any enquiry service evaluation.

Factual answers

- experience, education and training of the librarian;
- librarian's knowledge of and familiarity with the collection, services and facilities;
- adequacy and accessibility of the library collection;
- suitability of library policies;
- stress under which librarian is working;
- subject expertise.

Negotiating skills

- ability to communicate;
- decision-making skills;
- ability to unravel complex issues;
- ability to comprehend answers.

Attitudes

- willingness to communicate;

- perception of and commitment to professional responsibilities;
- status of the enquirer;
- personalities of interviewer and interviewee.

Provision of instruction

- ability to know when to instruct;
- ability to instruct;
- ability to know how much to include;
- ability to assess effectiveness of instruction.

HOW TO EVALUATE?

The methods used to evaluate readers' enquiry services will depend on the objectives of the exercise and the resources available in terms of staff time and money. As Cronin (1982) suggested there are two levels of investigation: (a) an analysis of the character and volume of use made of the service and facilities; and (b) an assessment of the quality, accuracy and competence of the service from the user's point of view. In practice a combination of these two should provide a realistic picture of the efficiency and effectiveness of the service.

Quantitative Evaluation

Some libraries will require only statistics either for their own management decision-making purposes or for other agencies who may wish to apply them for comparative purposes (Kesselman and Watstein, 1987). The first task is to clarify with the staff who are involved in the statistics gathering the definition and nature of a reader's enquiry. For example, should locational or directional questions be included? Should assistance with machinery be included?

Having clearly identified the type of enquiry, a count may be made in terms of the following:

- enquiries during a given period of time;
- enquiry duration, categorizing as short (under 5 minutes?) or long (over 5 minutes?) enquiries;
- enquiries at specific service points;
- users' faculty, department, course, mode of attendance etc.;
- category of question, for example fact finding, OPAC-based, subject based, database, referral etc.;

- sources used;
- form and content of answer.

Appendix IV shows an example of a simple reporting form used on reference enquiry points consisting of a simple five bar gate system.

When counting is carried out on a continuous basis, care should be taken to include all relevant enquiry transactions – those at various service points and offices where appropriate – to provide a more accurate view. Other counting periods may include quiet/busy times, quiet/busy floors or rooms, specific days, vacation periods. Alternatively, it may be necessary to collect the data by sampling. Sampling can be straightforward as long as the time periods chosen are truly representative. A more detailed explanation of sampling procedures is contained in Chapter 9.

At the end of the designated periods a statistical figure will be available to the librarian indicating the number of enquiries *dealt with*. Depending on the level of detail included in the categorization of enquiries, figures may also be available for types of users, questions, sources used, specific service points etc. However, what the figures will definitely not provide is a qualitative evaluation of the service's effectiveness.

Qualitative Evaluation

The two main methods which are adopted to satisfy Cronin's second set of criteria – the assessment of quality, accuracy and competence – are tests and surveys.

Tests

Since the mid-1960s unobtrusive testing has been carried out in both academic and public libraries to gauge the accuracy of factual responses to enquiries. A seminal paper by Webb (1966) discusses the merits of unobtrusive testing over other techniques. Childers (1987) questioned the success of this type of testing in making generalizations about the overall readers' enquiry process. In this type of testing, library staff are unaware they are being tested when dealing with an enquiry. Questions with predetermined answers are posed by 'proxies' who play the role of, say, a student and the testing team ensures the availability of the sources with which to find the required answers. After the enquiry interview the 'proxies' complete checksheets to report back on answers, attitudes, sources used etc.

Although the literature on unobtrusive testing is extensive, a number of criticisms have been levelled at this research, including the following issues. First, the method may only test one – some may say, a small – part of the whole reader's enquiry. Depending on the nature of the questions asked, negotiating and interviewing skills and decision-making techniques may not be required. It would be unfair to make a judgement of an enquiry service on this limited basis. Second, short, factual questions/responses, whilst easy to set, control and analyse, are unrealistic and unlikely to be representative of academic library enquiries. Such questions/responses also take no account of the information philosophy of many academic libraries of instructing users, where possible or appropriate, in search skills and techniques. This is an example of the methodology driving the objectives rather than vice versa. Third, some users may be satisfied with a partial or incomplete response to a question. Unobtrusive testing would undoubtedly treat such a response as a failure. Finally, Crowley (1985) emphasizes an ethical point: is it right to pose questions to library staff in the full knowledge that the event is stage-managed and false? Could this even be psychologically damaging to staff?

Whilst the above criticisms must be taken into account, unobtrusive testing may still be carried out but in conjunction with other methods to provide the complete picture. The arch exponents (Hernon and McClure, 1987a; 1987c) of this type of testing recognize its shortcomings in terms of incompleteness. Its advantages, however, lie in its success in gathering data from the perspective of the library users. Its attraction lies partly in its ability to provide 'hard' and quantifiable data (even if the data are measuring an unrepresentative element) rather than 'soft' and more subjective data.

Results of unobtrusive testing of enquiry services show a consistent pattern in both academic and public libraries – the so-called 55% rule. The indication is that more than four out of ten enquiries provide unsatisfactory responses. This figure, confirmed by Hernon and McClure (1987b) and Burton (1990), must surely be unacceptable in professional terms even taking into account the criticisms levelled at the method. Olszak (1991) has explored the reasons which lie behind the incidents of mistakes and failures by reference staff. Those who wish to consider the results of other unobtrusive testing exercises are referred to the Further Reading section at the end of the chapter.

Obtrusive testing is a variation on the above methods where the library staff are aware that the service is being tested. Results indicate a modest improvement in results. Most of the studies have been carried out in public libraries.

Satisfaction Surveys

In the field of readers' enquiries there seems to be a divergence of views on the value of satisfaction surveys. Van House *et al*. (1990) advocate a standard Reference Satisfaction Survey whilst Lancaster (1993) views their benefit with some scepticism preferring the more objective testing procedures referred to above. In the ideal world where time, staff and inclination are in abundance, a combination of the two methodologies (together with the quantifiable elements) – the hard, the soft and the statistical – could prove to be the most effective. This triangulation method represents a tried and tested social science research method providing an holistic approach. Appendix V shows a good example of a reference satisfaction survey sheet. Taken from Van House *et al*. (1990) this sheet provides an opportunity for those who have been involved in an enquiry to channel their views back to the Head of Library Services in order to improve the service ultimately. This particular example covers evaluation of the results of the enquiry and also the conduct and the attitude of the librarian. In this way it attempts to cover the process of the encounter rather than focusing only on the outcome as is the case with most unobtrusive testing.

When considering the results of this type of evaluation it must be borne in mind that users may be completely satisfied with the outcome (relevance, amount, completeness etc.) and the quality of service (helpfulness, approachability, attitude etc.) but the information may be inaccurate. Indeed, it may not be until after completing a questionnaire and leaving the library that the user realizes that the information received was not the information required. The questionnaire could reveal complete satisfaction with the process. This point gets to the heart of the problem of satisfaction surveys and one of the main reasons for adopting a cautious approach: their subjective nature. They represent the opinions of the participants in the process. The satisfaction levels of the library's users will depend greatly on their expectations of that service. Equally, expectations will be a product of educational and cultural backgrounds, personal and peer experiences in academic and other library services, and a multitude of other variables. An example of user satisfaction evaluation which includes comparisons between users' expectations and perceptions of actual service has been reported by Dalton (1992).

For optimum response rates questionnaires should be short, clear and unambiguous. They should be distributed at all appropriate service points by people trained in the art of polite and friendly persuasion. A decision should be made about:

1. The hoped-for number of responses. From this the approximate number for distribution is known based on an 80% response rate for previous readers' enquiry surveys.
2. The period during which the survey is to take place
3. Whether a sampling procedure is appropriate.

Other Methods

The success of a reader's enquiry may depend on a number of related elements, for example the extent of book and periodical collections, library policies, IT services and technical support, and the nature of the enquiry. However, the librarian will act as the fulcrum in balancing the above elements by not only applying negotiating and decision-making skills, search strategies and professional judgement but also bringing to bear on the enquiry the likelihood of a high level of expertise and a wealth of experience. The degree to which the librarian displays these facets can be assessed through the presence of a third party. A knowledgeable and experienced observer may be appropriate in such a situation as part of either the formal appraisal process or an informal developmental review (White, 1985). If feedback is provided in an open, mutually supportive and developmental way, the improvements in the service could be quite marked. This procedure would also provide the librarian with the opportunity to reflect upon his or her own performance.

FURTHER READING

Blandy, S. G., Martin, L. M. and Strife, M. L. (eds.) (1992) 'Assessment and accountability in reference work.' *Reference Librarian* **38** (17) special issue.

Dalton, G. (1988) 'Performance measurement matters when evaluating the effectiveness of reference services.' *Mousaion* **6** (2), 28–46.

Hernon, P. and McClure, C. R. (1987b) *Unobtrusive Testing and Library Reference Services.* Norwood, N.J.: Ablex Publishing.

Olson, L. M. (1984) 'Reference service evaluation in medium-sized academic libraries: a model.' *Journal of Academic Librarianship* **9** (6), 322–329.

Powell, R. R. (1984) 'Reference effectiveness: a review of research.' *Library and Information Science Research* **6**, 3–19.

Von Seggern, M. (1987) 'Assessment of reference services.' *RQ* **26** (4), 487–496.

Whitlatch, J. B. (1989) 'Unobtrusive studies and the quality of academic library reference services.' *College and Research Libraries* **50** (2), 181–194.

The following is a selection of examples of unobtrusive testing:

Bunge, C. A. (1985) 'Factors related to reference question answering success: the development of a data-gathering form.' *RQ* **24** (4), 482–486.

Elzy, C. A. (1991) 'Evaluating reference services in a large academic library.' *College and Research Libraries* **52** (5), 454–465.

McClure, C. R. and Hernon, P. (1983) *Improving the Quality of Reference Service for Government Publications.* Chicago: American Library Association.

Williams, R. (1987) 'An unobtrusive survey of academic library reference services.' *Library and Information Research News* **10** (37/38), 12–40.

CHAPTER EIGHT

Staff appraisal

JULIE PARRY

The starting point for an appraisal system should be the desire
to improve the performance of the library and to do that
requires improvement of the performance of individual members
of staff.

(Jones and Jordan, 1987, p.187)

When librarians begin to insist on their right to be appraised
then appraisal in academic libraries will have become a
progressive force capable of synthesizing the goals of both the
individual and the library organisation, to the benefit of both.

(Verrill, 1993, p.112)

The issues addressed in this chapter are:

- the purpose and benefits of appraisal;
- methods of assessing performance;
- the appraisal process;
- follow-up and evaluation.

Staff appraisal appears in several guises in academic institutions.
Although many organizations refer to performance appraisal or staff
appraisal schemes, there are those that carefully avoid the word
appraisal altogether, preferring terms such as 'staff review' and
'development'. However, regardless of the terminology, and the
operational variations that abound, appraisal is characterized by a
regular review of progress that focuses on the performance of individuals and/or the identification of development needs. In this, it
differs from other types of performance assessment, such as proba-
tion, which happen only once or on an irregular basis. There are
academic institutions which have implemented schemes that avoid

any hint of performance assessment, being solely concerned with the identification of training and development needs. Although such schemes fulfil a useful purpose they lack the satisfying completeness of an appraisal scheme that links past performance with future development.

BACKGROUND

Formal appraisal schemes were first developed in the United States during the 1920s. Initially, the emphasis was on psychological testing, and the principal purpose was to identify managers with development potential. However, by the end of the 1960s, a different approach was being advocated on both sides of the Atlantic. Instead of concentrating on the personality of individuals, the emphasis shifted to job performance. At the same time, the benefits of greater employee participation were being recognized and there was a move towards increased openness in reporting (Fletcher and Williams, 1992). Today's appraisal schemes have continued this trend, with self assessment and the identification of development needs featuring prominently in the better schemes.

Those who view appraisal in libraries as a relatively recent innovation may be surprised to learn that, 'attempts to rate and evaluate staff in an impersonal, objective and fair manner had begun in some American public libraries by the early 1920s' (Mole, 1980, p.99). Academic libraries in the United Kingdom have been rather more slow in rising to the challenge. Fielden (1993) found that only 57% of those institutions responding to a questionnaire had formal staff appraisal schemes for 'professional' library staff even though such schemes were mandatory for academic staff. Only 25% of those defined as 'non-professional' had a formal scheme. Perhaps not surprisingly, Verrill (1993, p.100) noted that

There is a great deal of suspicion and scepticism regarding performance appraisal, and librarians are no exception. For many people the term 'appraisal' carries with it connotations of control and rigidity. This view is reinforced by the Government's current enthusiasm for performance appraisal in the higher education sector and in the current climate many see the control factor as the overriding concern of appraisal systems.

Nevertheless, those who have participated in an effective appraisal scheme are generally supportive of the process and there are demonstrable benefits for both employers and employees.

THE PURPOSE OF APPRAISAL

The principal objectives of appraisal have been identified by ACAS (Advisory, Conciliation and Arbitration Service 1988, p.3) as follows:

- to review performance and identify how performance might be improved
- to review employees' potential and identify development needs
- to link performance with reward, for example performance-related pay

The schemes developed by different institutions may cover a whole range of objectives but most will be variations on those listed above. Yeates (1990) argues that performance and potential appraisal should not be linked in the same scheme, as each type of appraisal requires different skills. She also goes on to recommend that in schemes which link pay with performance, 'the system of measurement and link with the pay levels must be clear and defensible and appraisers must be very well trained in marking and defending the mark'(pp.38–39).

THE BENEFITS OF APPRAISAL

Services

Academic libraries exist to provide a range of information services to their parent institutions including those covered in Chapters 5–7. Improvements in service delivery require improvements in the performance of individual members of staff. If it is the aim of staff appraisal to improve the performance of employees then the performance of the library will benefit accordingly.

Performance

Performance may be improved by enabling individuals to identify their own strengths and weaknesses. Appraisal is an effective vehicle for encouraging staff to work with their managers to seek ways and means of tackling areas of weakness and of improving overall performance.

Communication

Even the best managers may fail, on occasion, to give their staff adequate feedback on work that has been done. In turn, employees may feel that their performance has been constrained by circumstances, but lack the will or the ability to draw the matter to the attention of senior staff. Appraisal offers managers and employees a formal opportunity to exchange views and discuss individual performance in the context of the library's strategic plans.

Motivation

Fletcher (1993, p.24) notes that 'setting targets is a powerful way of increasing motivation'. He goes on to explain that if staff are publicly committed to achieving goals that they participated in defining, their self-esteem will be bound up in attaining those goals. Formally acknowledging achievements by offering praise is another positive method of keeping motivation levels topped up.

Planning

Appraisal provides an ideal vehicle for ensuring that individual and organizational goals remain in harmony. Forward planning may also be helped. For example, staff training and development activities can be more effectively planned and coordinated if they are based on a systematic needs analysis.

DRAWBACKS

Naturally, there may be drawbacks as well as advantages. Institutions that try to introduce appraisal without adequate preparation or training may find considerable resistance, leading to suspicion and mistrust of the motives of senior management. Lack of clarity about the purpose of a scheme may cause confusion, leading to a low level of commitment. Raised expectations may be a problem if staff are led to believe that all their needs and wants will be satisfied but then find that nothing concrete actually happens. One of the main difficulties, however, is the amount of time involved in preparation, consultation, interviewing, writing reports and following up recommendations. The steadily increasing pressure being exerted on academic institutions and their library services has already made time a very precious commodity for library staff. Nevertheless, unless adequate time is made available for appraisal, it is unlikely that any of the benefits mentioned above will accrue.

METHODS OF ASSESSING PERFORMANCE

As long as the purpose of a scheme extends beyond the mere identification of training needs, some method of assessing performance will be necessary. This assessment will be a key element in the appraisal process and will provide a basis for discussion during the interview. Assessment techniques may be categorized as comparative, absolute or results-oriented. In comparative schemes the performance of individuals is ranked by a number of techniques, resulting in a ranking of employees from best to worst. Comparative methods have major drawbacks for library and information services in that they provide no qualitative information, they cannot be used to provide feedback and they are highly subjective. Absolute methods include narrative reports, rating scales and critical incidents. These and results-oriented methods have much more to offer and most schemes will combine elements from the two types.

Narrative report

A narrative report is a written statement which describes the appraisee's performance and behaviour. The extent to which the content of the report is prescribed will depend upon the nature of the scheme. For example, library staff following a scheme devised for academic staff may find that they are allowed considerable freedom of expression in completing the report. Naturally, the success of this approach rests heavily on written communication skills. Narrative reports may also be combined with rating scales.

Rating scales

Rating scales are systems in which appraisers grade appraisees under a number of categories. It may simply be a matter of ticking boxes or assigning letters or numbers to statements such as 'planning ability' or 'ability to communicate in writing'. Rating scales have the benefit of being relatively cheap and simple to administer as they do not require lengthy written reports. However, as they are

not linked to the specific requirements of a post they have a reputation for being over-subjective. The aim of the Behaviourally
Anchored Rating Scales (BARS) approach is to provide a rating
system which is linked (or anchored) to key performance aspects in
a range of jobs, thus reducing subjectivity in assessments.

Critical incidents

This method involves the appraiser noting examples of good and
poor performance over the period covered by the appraisal. These
'critical incidents' then form a basis for discussion. The benefits of
this objective approach, which is designed to focus on actual events
rather than personalities, are somewhat outweighed by the time and
effort required to watch continuously and to record what the
employee is doing.

Results-oriented methods

The essence of results-oriented or outcome-oriented methods is the
setting and measuring of objectives. Subjectivity on the part of the
appraiser is reduced as attention is focused on achievements rather
than on the personality or behaviour of the individual. These are
useful methods which encourage a participative approach through a
joint setting of objectives, leading to greater commitment by the
employee. It is important that, during appraisal, there is a fair exam-
ination of constraints and external circumstances that may have
affected the achievement of agreed targets. However, these methods
should be combined with others as they have certain weaknesses.
First, it may be difficult to set meaningful objectives for some types
of job. Second, the way in which someone behaves in their job may
in fact be extremely important. For example, oral communication
skills and approachability are important characteristics, particularly
for front-line reader services staff, that do not readily lend themselves to the setting of objectives.

WHO IS APPRAISAL FOR?

Ideally, staff on all grades should be involved. However, it is not
necessary for everyone to be appraised under identical schemes. For
example, librarians on academic or academic-related grades may
benefit from being appraised under the same scheme as teaching

staff. Such schemes often rely heavily on self-assessment and a fairly loosely structured narrative report. Library assistants, on the other hand, may feel more comfortable with a scheme that has been designed specifically for clerical staff. In this case the approach would be more prescriptive, with a higher degree of assessment by line managers. Jordan (1992) gives an account of an interesting approach to the appraisal of groups, as opposed to individuals, in recognition of the increased amount of teamwork in academic libraries.

WHO SHOULD ASSESS PERFORMANCE?

Performance has been traditionally assessed by immediate supervisors or line managers but there are a number of ways in which other staff can be involved.

Self-assessment

The use of self-assessment or self-appraisal has grown considerably in recent years. Some research has shown that self-assessment can lead to inflated self-evaluation and low correspondence with appraisals conducted by supervisors. Other research has indicated a tendency for people to underestimate their achievements. There is certainly evidence to support the view that employees and their supervisors generally hold significantly different views to each other but, unfortunately, there is no straightforward way of determining whose view is the more accurate (Long, 1986). In fact, this may not matter as there is little to be gained from a supervisor producing an accurate evaluation of an individual's performance if the person concerned fails to relate to that description and is resistant to suggestions about development or improvement. Library staff who have analysed their own performance are much more likely to take an active role in improving what they do than those who may disagree with their supervisor's point of view. Similarly, there will be more commitment to training and development from those who recognize their own needs than from those who are simply told of their weaknesses and sent on a remedial course. Effective schemes do not rely solely on self-appraisal, but use it in conjunction with other techniques such as peer appraisal.

Staff should not be expected to make a good job of self-appraisal without careful preparation and guidance. Preferably, all appraisees should receive training. In large organizations this may not be possible but some form of written guidance should be provided as a minimum. For example, the University of the West of England's Support Staff Appraisal Scheme offers a comprehensive set of notes to help each appraisee to prepare for the process. In addition all appraisees are offered a briefing session at which the purpose and the operation of the scheme are explained in detail. Those attending the sessions are given plenty of opportunity to ask questions and to discuss any concerns that they might have.

Peer appraisal

It is likely that appraisal by peers will grow in popularity. The current trend towards flatter organizational structures means that supervisors are responsible for increasingly large numbers of staff. In these circumstances there may be no alternative but to involve other people in the process. Anderson (1993) suggests that, despite a number of benefits that may derive from peer appraisal, it is generally felt to be more acceptable for developmental purposes than for evaluative purposes. However, initial mistrust may give way to willing participation, as Barker and Enright (1993) explain in their description of a peer review scheme at Imperial College Libraries. In this case half of the eligible appraisers declined to take part in the first year of operation, but two-thirds were prepared to participate the following year. Again, careful preparation and training are essential to ensure that assessment is objective and that working relationships are not soured by judgements based on personal prejudices.

Upward appraisal

Appraisal of managers by their subordinates is an activity that is not yet widespread in the United Kingdom but is growing in popularity in the United States. This is not a technique that many people would find easy and, obviously, it would be counter-productive for appraisal to jeopardize working relationships between managers and their staff. Therefore, assessments must be made anonymously. In order to preserve anonymity it is necessary for several people to appraise each manager. As a result, the administrative burden, arising from collating and analysing large amounts of paperwork, can make this quite a costly option.

Multi-source appraisal

Probably the most common method of gathering information for appraisal purposes is to use a selection of sources. This method is particularly appropriate in library and information services where staff often spend time working in different sections under different supervisors. For example, information about the performance of library assistants may be sought from counter supervisors, line managers, team leaders and other staff with whom they come into contact. For subject librarians it would be appropriate to seek the views of faculty staff, line managers and even students, if teaching sessions are evaluated.

PREPARATION AND ORGANIZATION

Participation

The most successful appraisal schemes are based on a participative approach, in which staff at all levels are involved. This holds true at each stage from the design of a scheme to its implementation and subsequent evaluation. An appraisal scheme that is simply dumped on employees without preparation or negotiation is unlikely to result in trust or commitment. Another factor that will add to the credibility of a scheme is support from the top, so senior library managers must be seen to be actively involved. Most library staff will find themselves subject to appraisal schemes that have been developed by their parent organization but opportunities for influencing their design or operation may still be possible. For example, if a new scheme is being developed or implemented library staff can offer to participate in the design and testing. Established schemes should be reviewed regularly so, by offering to take part in the evaluative process, library staff can ensure that their opinions are heard.

Aims and objectives of the scheme

It is essential that any appraisal scheme should set out to meet clearly defined aims and objectives. Failure to do so will lead to a lack of understanding by appraisers as well as by appraisees. Any sense of confusion is bound to lead to a lack of commitment to the scheme and the whole thing may be perceived as a waste of time. For example, a university might establish a scheme with the intention of reviewing achievements and improving performance through training and staff development. However, unless these aims are made explicit, some employees may assume that they are being assessed for promotion prospects or a pay rise and be somewhat less than willing to admit to weaknesses for fear of jeopardizing their chances of success. In addition, it will prove almost impossible to evaluate a scheme without stated aims and objectives against which to measure effectiveness.

Documentation and confidentiality

The amount of paperwork generated for appraisal indicates how time-consuming the whole process can be. The types of documents that might be produced or referred to include: information about the scheme, practical guidelines, job descriptions, CVs, preparatory notes, appraisal forms, feedback from others consulted, action plans and interview records

One concern often expressed is that of confidentiality. With so many documents involved it is essential that security is given a high profile. Everyone concerned should be aware of the sensitive nature of these papers. Preferably, one person should have control of all completed forms and keep them securely locked away, although each individual will probably wish to keep a copy of his/her own appraisal report. Any preparatory documents that do not need retaining should be shredded. Of course there is no point in hiding away action plans or performance objectives as these should be referred to during regular review sessions.

The schemes in use in many academic libraries require appraisers to produce written reports. It is increasingly common for these to be prepared using a word processor, and it may be possible to obtain standard forms on computer disks and to work electronically. If appraisal documents are stored in a computer database, confidentiality must again be protected. Under the terms of the Data Protection Act 1984 any employee has the right to see any personal information about them held on computer. This is unlikely to be an issue if appraisees already have access to their own appraisal records. However, steps must be taken to ensure that records cannot be accessed by anyone without the appropriate authority.

Training

As most people approach their first appraisal with some degree of trepidation, effective training is vital, both for appraisers and appraisees. Many staff who have supervisory or managerial responsibility still feel ill equipped to judge the performance of others. Similarly, most people find it difficult to be entirely objective about their own performance, tending to be either under- or over-critical in their personal assessment. However, the requisite skills can be learned and improved with practice.

An institution which recognizes the value of appraisal must be prepared to invest resources in order to get the best out of its scheme. Therefore, unless there is a skilled training officer available within the institution, an external trainer should be hired. It is important to use someone who is experienced in interpersonal skills training, who understands the higher education context and will have credibility with the staff to be trained.

Training for appraisers should result in a thorough understanding of the appraisal process. There should be an emphasis on practical skills such as questioning, listening and summing up. In addition, practice may be needed in assessment techniques such as work observation. Role play will allow appraisers to take risks and make mistakes in a safe environment without compromising real working relationships.

In order to gain the greatest benefit from the scheme appraisees also need to undertake careful preparation. First, they too will need to understand the aims of the scheme. Misunderstandings at this stage could undermine not only the appraisal scheme itself but also the fundamental working relationship between individuals and their managers. Second, an understanding of the processes involved will help to allay suspicion and the fear of surprises. Third, as already indicated, most people find it difficult to assess their own performance objectively and can benefit from constructive guidance and the opportunity to practise.

APPRAISAL INTERVIEWS

Monitoring performance, giving feedback and identifying training needs are all activities that competent managers should be undertaking on an ongoing basis. However, it is also useful to have a formal review process to enable those concerned to reflect more deeply on achievements and difficulties over a set period of time. An annual interview, backed up with interim meetings, is a fairly common way of achieving this aim. Appraisal interviews are potentially stressful occasions so it is important that both appraisers and appraisees are well prepared.

Preparation

Some schemes recommend that a pre-interview meeting should be arranged a week or two before the actual interview takes place. Such a meeting can fulfil the following functions:

- to check that the appraisee's preparation is progressing well;
- to agree arrangements such as the time and location of the interview;
- to agree an agenda for the interview;
- to begin to establish a positive tone for the proceedings.

This meeting should be kept fairly short and care should be taken that it does not begin to cover the same ground as the appraisal interview itself.

Physical environment

Careful preparation also involves organizing suitable accommodation. Conventional wisdom dictates that the interview should take place in 'neutral territory'. The reality in most libraries is that suitable neutral space is at a premium so appraisers have to make the best of any rooms and offices that are available. There is no shortage of advice about how to set up a room for interviewing so that the appraisee does not feel disadvantaged or ill-at-ease. Naturally, steps must be taken to prevent any interruptions so that full attention can be given to the appraisee.

Structure

One of the challenges of appraisal is to keep the interview to a sensible length of time. About an hour is a reasonable period to allow performance and development issues to be discussed. For more senior posts up to two hours may be necessary but, beyond that time, concentration begins to flag and key issues can get lost in a mass of minor details. It can be tempting to follow interesting lines of discussion or be difficult to persuade talkative appraisees to keep to the point, but structuring the interview can help the appraiser to manage the process more effectively. The following steps are characteristic of a well-managed appraisal interview:

- short settling down period;
- brief explanation of the structure of the interview;
- performance review, covering four or five key areas;
- identification of training and development needs;
- longer term aims;
- conclusion (preferably on a positive note).

Interview skills

All appraisers need a considerable range of skills. Ideally, these should be acquired during formal training and practised regularly. Interviewing skills are covered more generally in Chapter 9.

Questioning

Skilful questioning should result in the appraisee doing most of the talking. The appraiser may need to use a variety of questions to elicit useful information and to keep the interview progressing. Among the most useful types are open questions that require answers fuller than 'yes' or 'no', probing questions that examine what lies beneath superficial answers and reflective questions that summarize or paraphrase to check understanding. The type of questions to be avoided are leading questions in which the interviewer effectively provides the answer and multiple questions, in which two or more questions are wrapped up in one.

Listening

Inexperienced or poorly prepared interviewers may find themselves more concerned with framing the next question than with hearing the answer to the last one. Failure to listen carefully to what is being said can lead to misunderstandings and inaccurate reporting. In addition, the appraisee may be left with the impression that their appraiser is disinterested or incompetent, neither of which is a particularly desirable outcome.

Note taking

The appraiser should take notes upon which to base a written report of the interview. The purpose of the notes must be explained to the appraisees who should also be invited to take notes if they so wish. A verbatim record is not necessary at this stage but jotting down key words and phrases will be a help in maintaining accuracy. Any action plans or agreed objectives must be carefully recorded as they will form the basis of future activities and will be reviewed at the next appraisal interview.

Setting performance objectives

If performance objectives are to be of any value they must reflect organizational strategy, they must be attainable and there should not be too many of them. Objectives should be meaningful as there will be little challenge or sense of achievement if targets are set too low. At the same time, unrealistically high targets are likely to result in failure and demoralization. During an interview it can be easy to be over-optimistic about what might be achieved in the future but any list that exceeds six separate objectives is too long. Once again, a participative approach is recommended in which managers and their staff jointly identify and agree suitable objectives.

Giving feedback

Although members of staff have a need and a right to know how well they are performing, many managers find it particularly difficult to provide adequate feedback. It is important that both praise and criticism should be delivered as and when appropriate, throughout the year. Neither should be saved up and dropped on the unsuspecting appraisee during an appraisal interview. Constructive criticism can be particularly valuable, but it must be handled sensitively. This means examining problems objectively and using specific examples to illustrate the points being made. Criticism that is based on unsubstantiated evidence or personal prejudice will tend to make people react defensively, and if this happens it can be difficult to regain their confidence.

Summarizing

Time spent summarizing at the end of the interview will be time well spent. First, it gives the interviewer an opportunity to run through the interview notes while everything is still fresh in the mind. Second, it allows the appraisee to query any inaccuracies or omissions then and there. As a result, the written version is less likely to cause any surprises or give cause for dissent later on. While the aim of the process should be to reach a mutual understanding, it is perfectly legitimate for the appraisee to disagree with the assessment being made of their performance. If this is the case, the disagreement should be noted on the form.

Follow-up

As already noted, the appraisal interview is only one activity in the ongoing relationship between appraiser and appraisee. This is a good reason why the interview should be conducted in a constructive manner. It would be counter-productive if the exercise were to result in an irrevocably damaged working relationship. Ideally, appraisees should emerge from the interview feeling confident that their achievements have been recognized. They should also feel well motivated to address any areas of weakness that may have been identified. The appraiser has a continuing role to play in ensuring that the level of motivation does not drop and that agreed action plans are actually put into practice. In some organizations monthly meetings may be held to monitor progress. In others, an interim meeting between appraisals may be supplemented by less formal exchanges to make sure that progress is being maintained.

TRAINING AND STAFF DEVELOPMENT

In effective appraisal schemes improvements in performance may often be linked with training or staff development. However, wise managers do not make rash promises about training opportunities during the course of the interview. It is preferable to use the interview to identify the need but to decide how best to meet that need at a later stage. For example, if it were to become apparent during an interview that a subject librarian needed to develop online searching skills it would be unwise to make a commitment to an expensive external course without investigating different options, including in-house training.

The training and staff development needs of all staff, as identified throughout the appraisal process, should be brought together to form the basis of an annual training plan. This information is invaluable for those who manage staff development budgets and who seek to meet training needs in the most cost-effective way. Fears are sometimes expressed that the training costs arising from appraisal will be prohibitive. This need not be the case as long as appraisers understand how to draw up realistic sets of targets that do not necessarily rely on expensive training options.

EVALUATION

As discussed at the beginning of this chapter, one of the key purposes of appraisal is to assess how well an individual is performing in a job. Naturally, the effectiveness of the system which is established to conduct that process should also be assessed. Yeates (1990) recommends a process of validation and evaluation. Validation is concerned with finding out if the scheme is achieving its stated objectives and evaluation is concerned with the way in which the objectives are achieved. Yeates admits that validation is so difficult that many organizations avoid the challenge. On the other hand, evaluation studies can involve relatively straightforward questions concerning satisfaction levels of those concerned, consistency of approach and ways in which the scheme might need amending. Information may be obtained by conducting interviews or surveys or by analysing paperwork. Finally, a meaningful evaluation cannot be conducted without a clear set of objectives against which to measure the effectiveness of the scheme.

FURTHER READING

The following articles and chapters refer to staff appraisal in the context of library and information services:

Auckland, M. (1990) Training for staff appraisal. In Prytherch, R. (ed.). *Handbook of Library Training Practice*, Vol.2. Aldershot: Gower. pp. 90–112.

Berkner, D. (1983) Library staff development through performance appraisal. In Person, R. *The Management Process: a Selection of Readings for Librarians*. Chicago: American Library Association. pp. 327–341.

Casteleyn, M. and Webb, S. P. (1993) *Promoting Excellence: Personnel Management and Staff Development in Libraries*. London: Bowker Saur.

Cohen, L. R. (1989) 'Conducting performance evaluations.' *Library Trends* **38** (1), 40–52.

Gibbs, S. (1986) Staff appraisal. In Prytherch, R. (ed.) (1986) *Handbook of Library Training Practice*. Aldershot: Gower. pp. 61–81.

Green, A. (1993) 'A survey of staff appraisal in university libraries.' *British Journal of Academic Librarianship* **8** (3), 193–209.

Jones, N. and Jordan, P. (1987) *Staff Management in Library and Information Work* (2nd ed.). Aldershot: Gower.

Rizzo, J. R. (1980) *Management for Librarians: Fundamentals and Issues.* Westport, Cn.: Greenwood.

The following texts offer guidance and general practical advice on appraisal:

Anderson, G. C. (1993) *Managing Performance Appraisal Systems.* Oxford: Blackwell.

Fletcher, C. (1993) *Appraisal: Routes to Improved Performance.* London: Institute of Personnel Management.

Fletcher, C. and Williams, R. (1992) *Performance Appraisal and Career Development.* (2nd ed.). Cheltenham: Stanley Thornes.

Moon, P. (1993) *Appraising Your Staff.* London: Kogan Page.

Yeates, J. D. (1990) *Performance Appraisal: a Guide for Design and Implementation* (IMS Report No.188). Brighton: Institute of Manpower Studies.

CHAPTER NINE

Survey methods

Inevitably, there has been a tendency to use as indicators
measures which rely on data which are easy to collect and
manipulate.... relatively little attention has been paid to
qualitative measures.
(Joint Funding Councils' Libraries Review Group, 1993, p.32)

The issues covered in this chapter are:

- the evaluation techniques most widely used in reader services
  including:
    - questionnaires
    - interviewing
    - discussion groups
- the four factors which aim to ensure a rigorous approach in most
  evaluative situations:
    - sampling
    - piloting
    - validity
    - reliability

Within the social sciences there exists a bewildering array of
methodological advice about the most appropriate means of collecting, analysing and interpreting data. A number of such research
methods are applicable in librarianship and information studies. The
most widely applied methods for evaluation of library services
involve the use of surveys of one kind or another (Morgan, 1993).
Also indicated in the same survey is the difficulty of eliciting qualitative data in contrast to the quantitative kind which have been
predominant in the past. The evaluative processes covered in the

chapters on reader services often require the use of survey work. Examples might include the following:

- the distribution of a questionnaire following a user education session;
- a brief interview with library users who have been involved in a reader's enquiry;
- a general user satisfaction questionnaire distributed to every fifth person leaving the library;
- an availability survey (interview or questionnaire) asking whether users had indeed retrieved what they were looking for;
- a postal or telephone survey administered to a sample of students and academic staff requesting their views on particular aspects of the service, for example the interlibrary loans service, service to part-time students etc.;
- a discussion group of students, academic staff and librarian trying to find ways of improving aspects of the service, for example the Short Loan Collection, audiovisual facilities etc.

Generally, the aim of surveys is to find out factual, behavioural or attitudinal information. Therefore, for the purposes of this chapter emphasis will be placed on survey work, with an attempt to bring together and synthesize the main considerations when embarking on this group of methods. Those wishing to explore the myriad of other techniques available within library service evaluation are referred to a range of sources listed in the Further Reading section. Also in the literature of library and information studies references are made to user studies. Having consulted many of these, the present author and many others have been unable to distinguish satisfactorily between user studies and user surveys. They appear to be synonymous. For the reader who wishes to explore the various studies/surveys carried out in recent decades and discussions on methods and results, the books by Ford (1977) and Powell (1988) are thoroughly recommended. Each contains a bibliography of over 200 entries. Powell, in particular, discusses the possible benefits and limitations of performance measures based on user studies.

QUANTITATIVE VERSUS QUALITATIVE METHODS

Initially it would be beneficial to compare and contrast these two methodological perspectives. Although surveys may belong in both camps, their practical application is likely to differ in accordance with the particular views of the researcher or evaluator. Table 9.1 provides a rather simplistic and crude summary of characteristics of each model.

Table 9.1 Quantitative versus qualitative characteristics

Quantitative	Qualitative
Breadth/mass data	Depth/smaller samples
Objective	Subjective
'Scientific'	'Non-scientific'
Highly structured approach	Looser approach
Answers 'how often?' – statistical	Answers 'why?' – causative
Less helpful with complex topics	More helpful with complex topics
Emphasis on neutrality	Emphasis on the actor's perspective
Usually clear-cut precise results	Useful for preliminary work

The quantitative versus qualitative debate has been the source of a continuing dialogue within the academic research community – in terms of validity, reliability, rigour, personal preference or just simple prejudice. Although this is not the place to enter the debate on positivistic and naturalistic methods, for those seeking further background details on these and other approaches to social science methodologies, the books by Blaikie (1993) and Erlandson et al. (1993) are recommended.

Quantitative

The quantitative model usually uses large study samples drawn rigorously according to statistically valid methods. Many practitioners deem this model to be more objective and 'scientific', and therefore to provide better results. Validity and reliability are considered later in this chapter. Whilst these points may be matters for discussion, quantitative measures do tend to be highly structured and controlled through the use of questionnaires or interview schedules. For example, heavy reliance is placed on checklists, tick boxes, 'yes'/'no' responses with little allowance for flexibility. The quantitative model is generally applied effectively to, say, availability/failure studies, frequency of library visits or usage of particular services. Such studies inevitably involve statistical and/or mathematical analysis to reveal trends or patterns. For exploration of topics of some complexity, quantitative methods can be less helpful. The main priority of this set of methods is objectivity wherever possible. Recommended reading for explanation and application of statistical methods in librarianship is the book by Hafner (1989), which is particularly helpful for those who lack a background in statistical methods.

Qualitative

Qualitative methods really come to the fore when the evaluation requires in-depth exploration of specific issues. For example, a general satisfaction survey which seeks a 'yes'/'no' response to the question 'are you satisfied with the level of service provided?' would be very limiting. If the results are to be more meaningful, the survey needs to probe the respondent to gain further insights and perhaps get to the heart of the issue. Since in-depth probing can be time consuming and labour intensive, smaller samples will tend to be drawn. These so-called non-'scientific' and subjective measures provide a plethora of information, perhaps in the form of transcriptions of tape recordings or details taken from open questions on self-administered questionnaires. Whilst analysis and interpretation may throw up barriers and difficulties, the consequent results should reflect the participant's perspective. It has been suggested that this looser approach tends to provide information that is enlightening for policymakers (Robson, 1993) without the inhibiting precursor of assumptions and expectations which may be built into highly structured tick boxes. This tendency to illumination represents a strength that is effective in dealing with complex research or evaluation situations in which reason and causality are sought.

Although quantitative and qualitative measures have been divided here for the sake of convenience, it should be remembered that they may live in harmony and complement each other. Here are two examples which illustrate the point.

Example 1
A questionnaire is distributed to all 150 students who participated in a user education session. The questionnaire is short but structured and requests 'yes'/'no' and tick responses. Subsequent analysis shows that the majority are less than satisfied with the content of the session and indeed with the method of instruction. The librarian needs further insights into the reasons for the dissatisfaction and therefore interviews are arranged with a sample of participating students. Hopefully, improvements which will benefit subsequent user education programmes, are likely to result from these interviews.

Example 2
It becomes clear that the interlibrary loans service has come under extreme pressure from the volume of transactions. The head of library service decides to interview senior library staff to discuss the problem and possible solutions. Issues for discussion revolve around student numbers, more project work, decreasing funds, more information-skills teaching, more extensive use of a wider range of IT services etc. Possible solutions revolve around charging (either through subsidizing or in full), limiting (by number, category of user etc.), altering funding arrangements, provision of extra staffing, consideration of cooperative schemes and document delivery services etc. The librarian then sets in train, amongst other things, a wide survey of other higher education libraries to find out to what extent the problems of borrowing from other sources exist in other libraries and what solutions have been found.

Both examples illustrate how particular methods may be adopted to suit the nature of the enquiry. The justification for applying either quantitative or qualitative methods lies in the ultimate effectiveness in providing satisfactory results.

QUESTIONNAIRE SURVEYS

In order to help in deciding whether to use a questionnaire survey, Table 9.2 provides a list of some advantages and disadvantages of this method. Often extraneous issues such as resources, time and staffing may outweigh any of these considerations. The most signif-

icant factors in the questionnaire survey are its applicability in a
large scale evaluative exercise, its consistency of questioning (this
may be a problem with particularly inexperienced interviewers) and
the tendency for respondents to exercise their critical faculties when
there is distance between researcher and respondent or when
anonymity is promised.

Table 9.2 Questionnaire survey: advantages and
disadvantages

Advantages	Disadvantages
Ability to reach large sample numbers	Inadequacy in terms of complex or causal issues
Fixed format provides consistency of questioning	Little contact between researcher and respondent
Provides for anonymity	Potential for antagonism
Its construction should allow for ease of analysis of quantitative data	Difficulty in obtaining responses from a representative cross-section
Relatively short time span	Variable response rate
May allow respondents to reply in own time	
Respondents likely to be more critical than face-to-face	

Some of the disadvantages may take on great significance in certain circumstances. Questions about the ways in which students
make use of library services or the views of the users on ways of
improving services and facilities are difficult to answer by structured questionnaires. It is possible, but not necessarily desirable, to
leave plenty of space for open-ended questions in which respondents have the opportunity to expand their views. Experience
suggests that too many such questions merely antagonize the
respondents.
The second advantage highlights the importance of validity and

piloting so that the implications of this distance between evaluator and respondent are minimized. Once the questionnaire reaches the respondent's hands, it is often impossible to be in a position to clarify ambiguities unless the evaluator or researcher is present when the questionnaire is administered and completed.

One should never underestimate the questionnaire's potential to antagonize the respondents. A combination of diverse elements in one questionnaire may well push a respondent into a mood of irritability and refusal to cooperate. Such elements could be poorly worded questions, an illogically structured sequence of questions, badly designed layout, very little 'white space', cluttered appearance, excessive length, preponderance of open or closed questions, biased or leading questions etc. The fewer there are of these kinds of irritations, the greater will be the likelihood of meaningful and plentiful responses. As Oppenheim (1992, p.122) rightly points out, '...the respondent is doing us a favour by taking time and trouble to answer our questions'.

QUESTIONNAIRE DESIGN

Again Oppenheim (1992, p.100) is able to provide the essence of the questionnaire in the following extract:

A questionnaire is not some sort of official form, nor is it a set of questions which have been casually jotted down without much thought. We should think of the questionnaire as an important instrument of research, a tool for data collection. The questionnaire has a job to do: its function is measurement.

There may be some overlap when discussing questionnaires and interviews since the same sequence of questions may be administered in both situations. However, for the sake of convenience, these methods will be separated here and the problems inherent in each method will be explored under appropriate headings.

Questionnaires may be employed in standardized interviews; they may be administered by post, telephone or self-administered. The particular method will be chosen to suit the purpose. The structure and layout of the questionnaire should be designed to maximize the quality of the content and the number of responses. As the above extract indicates the application of this assessment method must be carefully planned and piloted, and appropriately administered.

An effective questionnaire is carefully structured so that the respondent is put at ease early in the process, with perhaps a general question that whets the appetite and motivates the respondent to proceed further. Any personal details, if required at all, should be requested near the end of the questionnaire with an accompanying explanatory sentence. Depending on the scope and nature of the topic under discussion, questions tend to proceed from the general to the specific – the so-called funnel approach. If the questionnaire contains a number of 'question modules' covering a particular variable of the topic, then each module tends to proceed likewise from the general to the specific. It is important that the sequencing of questions is transparent, logical and, if possible, interesting. Relations between questions and modules should be equally logical. Occasionally, it is necessary to provide routing instructions for the respondent to go to a later question; for example, 'if the answer is NO, please go to question 8'. Such filter questions are best avoided whenever possible since they can give the questionnaire the unwelcome appearance of clutter and complexity.

Designing any questionnaire is a delicate balancing act which endeavours to:

- avoid excessive length (leading to non-response or respondent fatigue);
- include all the relevant questions;
- include enough 'white space' so that the questionnaire can 'breathe';
- include questions of interest to encourage further participation;
- ensure consistency of instructions, for example ticking, circling etc.

CLOSED VERSUS OPEN QUESTIONS

Most questionnaires – and indeed interview schedules – contain a mix of closed (or precoded) and open (or free response) types of question. An open question provides the respondent with the freedom to answer spontaneously in his/her own words without being offered any kind of choice. A closed question is one where the respondent is offered a choice of answers – to be ticked, circled etc. An example of a closed question is:

How often do you visit the library? (Please tick)

More than once a day	_____
Once a day	_____
Twice a week	_____
Once a week	_____
Other	_____

An example of an open question is:

Do you have any comments to make about the enquiry service you received today?

_____

_____

_____

_____

Table 9.3 Closed versus open questions: advantages and disadvantages

	Advantages	Disadvantages
Open	1. Freedom to create detailed response 2. Provides opportunity to investigate complex events 3. A 'richer' picture and useful source of quotation	1. Time-consuming to answer, analyse and interpret 2. Diverse terminology for same things
Closed	1. Quick to answer 2. Easy to process	1. Possibility of bias 2. Sometimes crude and simplistic

Table 9.3 shows some of the advantages and disadvantages of each question type. From the respondent's viewpoint a combination of both types is likely to provide variety and motivation. Sometimes both types will appear in the same question, for example:

Did you find the content of the information skills programme relevant to your dissertation preparation?

YES _____   NO _____

If the answer is NO, could you suggest ways in which
the content may be improved?

_____

_____

_____

_____

Opinions are divided on the adoption of a middle alternative in
some closed questions. For example, these two questions are taken
from a survey following a user education session:

1. How clearly was the information presented in the
library session?

Very clearly   _____
Fairly clearly   _____
Not very clearly   _____
Unclearly   _____

2. Do you think the method of library instruction was a
good way of learning how to use the library?

A very good way   _____
A good way   _____
No feelings either way   _____
A poor way   _____
A very poor way   _____

In the first example the respondent is requested to choose between
'two sides of a coin'. There is no middle ground. In the second example
the respondent may choose to be noncommittal. According to Robson
(1993, p.248) 'typically, 20 per cent of respondents may use the middle
category but it appears that its inclusion or exclusion does not affect
the relative proportions of those actually expressing opinions'.

QUESTION WORDING

Much has been written about the importance of appropriate wording
of survey questions. If the questionnaire is to act as an accurate

measuring device, there are some simple guidelines which surveyors may follow:

Language
Survey designers should try to ensure that the language is simple, free of jargon and acronyms and that the words are likely to be familiar to potential respondents. Words such as catalogue, Dewey, sources, journal, index, OPAC, UDC etc may cause some confusion. It is easy to slip into the kind of language adopted for writing reports or official documents. Examples of such words are assist (= help), consider (= think), reside (= live), terminate (= end). Where possible respondents need to feel comfortable and at ease with the expressions and language of the questions. The aim is, therefore, for the language to be as close as possible to everyday language.

Sentences
The longer and more complex the questions are, the greater will be the likelihood of an inaccurate response or no response. It is more appropriate to ask complex questions through other means, for example interview or discussion where probing the issues is easier. Alternatively, the question may benefit from being disentangled and divided into two or three separate questions. Clarity may thus be preserved.

Ambiguity
The respondent must be absolutely clear about the precise meaning of the questions since no clarification or elaboration may be available, particularly if the questionnaire is self-administered, distributed through the post or sent out via e-mail. Typical ambiguities are illustrated in the following questions:

> Have you borrowed books or periodicals within the last week?
>
> Borrowing of periodicals should not be allowed.
> AGREE_____   DISAGREE_____
>
> How many library books have you read this week?
>
> Do you make regular use of the interlibrary loans service?
>
> Do you use the interlibrary loans service frequently?
>
> Do you think it's a good idea to include periodicals, discussion papers and monographs in the bulletin?

Have you used the library in the last week?

All these questions would benefit from being reworded to improve clarity. They include double-barrelled questions, double negatives and ambiguous words such as 'regular', 'frequently', 'use' and 'read'. An interesting piece of research by Bookstein (1982) explored library surveys in terms of the words used to describe library activities. The study suggested that the degree of variation in how people interpret the simplest terms is quite considerable.

INTERVIEWING

The interview is a kind of conversation; a conversation with a purpose.
(Robson, 1993, p.228)

Interviewing is a widely accepted and frequently adopted method of data collection in the social sciences. Much of the advice given for the administration of questionnaires applies equally to the interview situation. However, the presence of the spoken word introduces a dimension which has the potential to compromise the pursuance of rigour. But first, what are the advantages and disadvantages of the interview method? Table 9.4 shows a number of strengths particularly in terms of its suitability for addressing topics in depth and its potential for explanation and clarification. However, it is generally believed that the job of interviewing is a fairly straightforward one; is it not just having a purposeful conversation? The opposite is in fact the case. Interviewing requires training in the technique itself and in wider interpersonal skills so that uniformity, consistency and hence reliability are maintained. Its weaknesses may also include costs and time, together with difficulties of transcribing tape-recorded conversations and analysing and interpreting large amounts of data.

Interviewing usually falls into three categories which can be viewed on a continuum from the structured (formal, standardized) through the semi-structured (focused, guided) to the unstructured (free style, in-depth, informal, non-directive). In many ways the structured interview bears a close resemblance to the verbal administration of a questionnaire. Questions are predetermined, very often closed or of the checklist variety. The presence of the interviewer ensures that any necessary explanation and clarification may be given.

Table 9.4 Interviewing: advantages and disadvantages

Advantages	Disadvantages
Suitable for in-depth probing	Training required
More effective explanation of rationale	Difficulty in uniformity and consistency of questioning
More effective for dispelling ambiguity and helping clarification	Problem of accurate recording and transcription of data
Non-verbal responses helpful	Costly and time consuming

An example of the structured type of interview is a user study in which respondents are asked about the success (or otherwise) of their library visit. In this example, the interviewer circles the appropriate number.

Looked for library material	0	1	2	3	4
Studied	0	1	2	3	4
Did a literature search	0	1	2	3	4
Asked at enquiry desk	0	1	2	3	4
Browsed	0	1	2	3	4
Returned books	0	1	2	3	4
Other ...	0	1	2	3	4

0 = did not do today
1 = successful visit
4 = unsuccessful visit

Further along the continuum the semi-structured interview includes a worked-out set of points which may be explored appropriately during the interview. The questions are more likely to be of the open-ended variety. The structured straightjacket has been loosened. An example of the semi-structured type is separate interviews with a sample of individuals who had participated in a user education session. In this example, the interviewer needs to gauge the satisfaction levels of students on the following points:

1. method of instruction
2. practical exercises if used
3. content of programme
4. length of programme
5. feedback opportunities

At the other end of the continuum is the unstructured interview which tends to proceed in an informal way and covers an area of interest, but without specific predetermined questions. It resembles more a conversation, with the respondents taking overt control and the interviewer interjecting only when the discussion digresses too widely. An example of the unstructured type is an interview arranged with individual library users studying on a part-time postgraduate course. In order to provide future library support, particularly for non-traditional courses, it is helpful to find out students' views on the value of various aspects of the service with the aim of modification and improvement. This exercise provides an opportunity to explore respondents' experiences and reactions.

A number of skills and qualities are essential for the interviewer regardless of the type of interview; these include honesty, accuracy and interest. The depth and variety of such skill requirements increase as one travels along the continuum. In the structured interview the questions are administered using clear straightforward tones with maximum uniformity and consistency. The ability to deal with responses which may be inadequate, partial, irrelevant or inaccurate is a particular requirement. Further along the continuum the use of wider interpersonal skills becomes necessary, as the potential for interview bias increases and the interviewer becomes more involved in the discussion. Particularly in the case of the inexperienced interviewer, there may be a tendency to speak rather more than listen. It is important that the interviewees do most of the talking!

To carry out an unstructured interview effectively demands a high degree of skill. Various techniques are available to probe for further details in a non-threatening and trusting environment, to engage the respondent's interest and attention and to sustain a rapport throughout the interview. The ability to maintain a simultaneous distance and closeness, to remain detached and professional whilst exhibiting a relaxed and friendly manner are skills which take time to acquire and nurture.

PILOTING

Having devised a suitable survey questionnaire either for interview or distribution, there may be an almost overwhelming desire to enter directly into the data collection stage. This should be firmly resisted. The data collection device will almost certainly be improved in some way if pretested or given an experimental run. Not only will piloting produce a more effective measuring instrument, it will also promote efficiency in terms of time saved and frustration averted. Since surveys, and interviews in particular, can be expensive to administer, any possible savings are to be welcomed.

Although the advice about survey design given in this chapter has been limited to the essentials, a number of books on research methods (a number of which are listed in the Further Reading section) display a formidable range of tips and handy hints for the potential surveyor. One sure way of testing all this sometimes contradictory information is by piloting.

Pilot work involves the revision, refinement and in some cases reconstruction of the survey instrument so that the quality and quantity of the collected data are of the highest possible order. The piloting process is an iterative one in which alterations and modifications are continually tested and retested until no further fine-tuning is possible.

Ideally, piloting should be directed at a group similar in composition to the sample being surveyed in the main exercise. For example, if a user satisfaction survey were being carried out among 500 university library users, a sample of 50 would be drawn applying the same criteria as in the main exercise. As a rule of thumb 10% is considered to be appropriate. The survey would be carried out and feedback elicited on problems, ambiguities, unclear questions etc. Often more informal methods of piloting are applied before the above process. This may take the form of a peer group discussion in which it is not necessary for the participants to be familiar with the survey topic, and indeed it may be an advantage for the participants to approach the exercise from an objective and possibly 'fresh' viewpoint. Advice regarding the use of expert opinion is generally agreed to be essential, but it is no substitute for pilot work and should never be used as a short cut. Any expert advice on survey design should also form part of the piloting process.

Piloting, if it is to be effective, needs to cover comprehensively the data collection instrument. The main areas which require testing are these:

- wording and order of the questions;
- balance between open and closed questions;
- adequacy of multiple choice options;
- clarity of instructions and guidelines;
- content of the questions;
- questionnaire layout;
- interviewer style;
- appropriateness of tone/style;
- appropriateness of length;
- appropriateness of timing;
- overall structure;
- administration of the survey.

Perhaps most importantly, do the responses tell you what you need to know?

SAMPLING

Unless a particular survey is to include all possible elements, then a sample needs to be drawn. A sample is a subset which represents a larger group or target population. If truely representative, this subset resembles a microcosm of the larger group. The key concept which surrounds the whole area of sampling is representation – the so-called 'search for typicality' (Smith, 1975, p.105). Sampling may be appropriate if the following are being assessed:

- reference enquiry services;
- effectiveness of user education sessions;
- delay in document delivery;
- availability of books;
- level of satisfaction with library visit;
- usage of a particular service during specific time periods.

If the results of the performance assessment of any academic library activity are to be more generally applicable – perhaps in other contexts, situations or times, or indeed to people other than those involved – it is important that the sample is drawn with care and is suited to the purposes of the survey. Often generalizability as a result of performance assessment is undesirable. However, when it is, the credibility of the exercise's whole methodology may be put in jeopardy through poor sampling techniques.

Difficulties may arise when considering the size of a particular sample, since this is more a matter of judgement rather than statistical correctness. Accuracy and representativeness are more likely to determine the sample's effectiveness. As an incidental point, an unnecessarily large sample will have resource implications in terms of data collection and analysis. The margin of error in the results of a sample of 2000 may be around 2% either way. Using a sample size of 200 it may be 6%. Such estimates are dependent on other factors including an appropriate and up-to-date sampling frame, no non-responses, numbers of subgroups surveyed etc. In the end time and money may be the main criteria for the sampling process.

A fleeting glance in any standard statistics textbook will indicate the complex and highly technical nature of sample selection. Without wishing to discourage the statistical explorer, for small-scale survey work the advice given by Oppenheim (1992) or Robson (1993) is sufficient. The Further Reading section provides some titles that are more advanced.

Main Sampling Techniques

There are four main sampling techniques pertinent to assessment methods in academic libraries.

Simple Random Sample
This involves the random selection of the desired number from the sampling frame, for example the complete list of books, students, interlibrary loan requests etc. Here randomness indicates a statistically defined procedure requiring random number tables (these are available in many statistics textbooks) or computer-generated random numbers. Such a process ensures that each individual item (or person) has an equal chance of being selected.

Systematic Sampling
This involves selecting a starting point in the sampling frame and then each nth item (or person). A sample which requires 300 students from a sampling frame of 9000 means that every 30th person is chosen. The starting point would need to be randomly selected between 1 and 30.

Stratified Random Sampling

This involves dividing the sampling frame into different strata, for example books in a classification scheme or library users by faculty or department. Random sampling then takes place within each of the strata. Proportionate sampling would be appropriate in ensuring that the numbers for each stratum reflect the relative numbers in the sampling frame. For example, a satisfaction survey dealing with library opening hours which aims to represent the total library user population may require its sample to be divided proportionately between academic staff, full time students, part time students, access/franchise students, short course students etc. In this example concern about those who do not make use of the library service is an important but separate issue.

Convenience (or Accidental) Sampling

This involves the sample items (or persons) being chosen at the convenience of the person drawing the sample. Robson (1993, p.140) regards this method as 'a cheap and dirty way of doing a sample survey. It does not produce representative findings'. Paradoxically, this technique is employed widely and reported in the literature, thus negating or seriously compromising some assessment strategies. The term 'accidental' contains a misleading connotation of randomness. The tendency for selection bias and other extraneous influences is almost inevitable. Its usage should really be confined to assisting in piloting questionnaires or 'getting a feel' for a topic or area of research.

Finally, sound advice is to incorporate the sampling procedure in the pilot exercise.

VALIDITY AND RELIABILITY

Although it is unnecessary to dwell at length on these two interrelated concepts the value and trustworthiness of any performance assessment exercise are enhanced through the validity and reliability of methods, instruments, data and results.

Validity is concerned with the extent to which the assessment methods used actually measure what they set out to measure. Are questions answered truthfully? Are attitudes or views displayed in an interview borne out by subsequent behaviour? Can a respondent recall accurately some library event, number of visits, items read/borrowed etc? What may be even more difficult to deal with is the validity of results. Are the analysis and interpretation of collected data a valid representation of the results? Are purported causal relationships true? Is it a true picture of the service or facility under scrutiny? These are matters of internal validity. One has to be forever vigilant, strive for objectivity and be constantly aware of the boundaries and limitations of the exercise from instrument design to reporting of results or conclusions. External validity may be synonymous with generalizability in that appropriate sampling procedures have to be chosen and carried out. In this way the value of the exercise is further enhanced.

In the context of survey work reliability refers to the use of stable, consistent and dependable methods, instruments, questions and exercises. Could the exercise be repeated in the full confidence that similar results would be produced? Many unreliable factors which can creep into questionnaires or interview schedules may be eliminated through assiduous pilot work. This essential stage allows for a more rigorous approach to rooting out any carelessness or casualness.

Issues of validity and reliability are addressed in more detail by Kirk and Miller (1986) and Shipman (1988).

FURTHER READING

Baker, S. L. and Lancaster, F. W. (1991) *The Measurement and Evaluation of Library Services* 2nd (ed.). Arlington, Va.: Information Resources Press.

Beed, T. W. and Stimpson, R. J. (1985) *Survey Interviewing*. London: Unwin Hyman.

Busha, C. H. and Harter, S. P. (1980) *Research Methods in Librarianship: Techniques and Interpretation*. New York: Academic Press.

Hafner, A. W. (1989) *Descriptive Statistical Techniques For Librarians*. Chicago: American Library Association.

Henry, G. T. (1990) *Practical Sampling*. London: Sage

Kalton, G. (1983) *Introduction to Survey Sampling*. London: Sage

Kirk, J. and Miller, M. L. (1986) *Reliability and Validity in Qualitative Research*. London: Sage

Line, M. B. and Stone, S. (1982) *Library Surveys: An Introduction to The Use, Planning, Procedure and Presentation of Surveys*. London: Clive Bingley

Marsh, C. (1988) *Exploring Data: An Introduction to Data Analysis For Social Scientists*. Cambridge: Polity Press

Martyn, J. and Lancaster, F. W. (1981) *Investigative Methods in Library and*

Information Science: An Introduction. Arlington, Va.: Information Resources Press.

Moser, C. A. and Kalton, G. (1971) *Survey Methods in Social Investigation.* (2nd ed.). London: Heinemann.

Oppenheim, A. N. (1992) *Questionnaire Design, Interviewing and Attitude Measurement.* London: Pinter.

Powell, R. R. (1985) *Basic Research Methods for Librarians.* Norwood, N.J.: Ablex Publishing.

Powell, R. R. (1988) *The Relationship of Library User Studies to Performance Measures: A Review of The Literature.* (Occasional Paper No.181). Illinois: University of Illinois Graduate School of Library and Information Science.

Robson, C. (1993) *Real World Research: A Resource For Social Scientists and Practitioner-Researchers.* Oxford: Blackwell.

Shipman, M. (1988) *The Limitations of Social Research* (3rd ed.). London: Longman.

Slater, M. (ed.) (1990) *Research Methods in Library and Information Studies.* London: Library Association Publishing.

Stone, S. and Harris, C. (1984) *CRUS Guide 1 Designing a User Study: General Research Design.* Sheffield: Centre for Research on User Studies.

CHAPTER TEN

Performance assessment: the way forward

GEOFFREY FORD

Perhaps the greatest management challenge will be to find ways
of applying what is an intellectually complex framework without
losing sight of the need to retain a strong element of common
sense and conventional wisdom.

(McLean and Wilde, 1991, p.210)

The aim of this final chapter is to pull together some of the threads
of the previous chapters, explore the latest developments in performance assessment being pursued by the Standing Conference of
National and University Libraries (SCONUL) and gain some insight
into the future use of performance indicators. The following related
issues are covered:

- the influence of external agencies;
- user involvement and feedback;
- information technology and management information;
- the continuing quest for standards;
- staff participation;
- planning;
- the SCONUL approach.

The 'charter' movement in the UK, alluded to in Chapter 2, has
had an impact on all public services, even where no formal charter
exists, so that managers are becoming much more explicit about
their response to user needs. At the same time, and not just in the
UK, the market model of service provision is increasing in influence: privatization or contracting out of services, market testing and
purchaser/provider relationships are the outcome of questioning the
view that public ownership, funding and management are necessarily the best ways of providing services for the public good.

Proposals for new developments are accompanied by business plans. Even where no money changes hands, 'gentlemens' agreements' are giving way, not to 'persons' agreements', but to service level agreements which provide explicitly for the evaluation of performance. In many universities, transparent cost allocation and resource allocation models, often accompanied by devolution of budgetary control, often lead to demands for detailed justification of decisions formerly made by hunch, or the exercise of judgement honed by experience. These trends will continue.

THE INFLUENCE OF EXTERNAL AGENCIES

Prompted by government, the HE funding councils in the UK have increasingly targeted funds which were formerly devoted to the general support of higher education. A division has been made between the support for teaching and the support for research. Explicit formulae relate the funding for research to the results of the research assessment exercise (Universities Funding Council 1992), and there is a widespread belief that in future the funding for teaching will likewise be related to the ongoing teaching quality assessment. These external evaluations are forcing institutions to be more explicit in defining their procedures, not only (and often for the first time) to their own staff and students, but also to the outside world. The importance of the Further Education Funding Council, particularly its cycle of inspection visits, is highlighted in Chapter 4.

There are several such external evaluations wherein the library's role will be increasingly important. The first of these relates to the procedures for quality assurance. In these assessments, the arrangements for liaison between a library and its users are important. The reports of these assessments are published, and it must be a salutary experience to read such statements as:

While fully recognising the complexity of a three-tier library system ... the audit team was not confident that the University could assure itself that, in a climate of increasing pressures on resources, present coordinating procedures were adequately meeting the future learning needs of its students. The team would encourage the University in its debates and consultations on this important matter.

(Higher Education Quality Council, 1993, p.24)

A second type of external evaluation is concerned with the assessment of teaching quality. There are a range of topics to which the institution needs to give attention:

- the arrangements for liaison with users;
- evidence of users' opinions of the library services;
- the responsiveness of the institution in remedying identified deficiencies;
- the extent and nature of innovation in provision of learning resources.

A third set of external evaluations involve professional bodies, such as the Law Society or the Royal College of Veterinary Surgeons, or other educational bodies which have a role in validating or accrediting courses of education and training. Such bodies may have explicit guidelines or standards against which a library is judged. For example, the Society of Public Teachers of Law issues a minimum statement of library holdings, and the Law Society has produced a draft list of library holdings necessary to support legal practice courses. Although this practice is not new, it is spreading as educational institutions are rapidly seeking and entering partnerships, validating, accrediting and franchising courses. Assessment of learning resources, often by librarians, is an essential part of these processes. In the field of postgraduate medical education, a set of guidelines for the accreditation of medical libraries has been produced (Committee of Postgraduate Medical Deans, 1993), and these have been adapted by SCONUL for general use.

From a library's point of view the parent institution is the funding agency: the more forward looking institutions are assessing their own activities in increasingly rigorous ways, and such internal reviews will become more common. The guidelines used at one university set out the following objectives:

1. to help the library to identify and evaluate strengths and weaknesses in its support of teaching and learning, research and scholarship, and in the management of the enterprise within the pattern of existing resources;
2. to help the library to identify and evaluate strengths and weaknesses in its organization and management;
3. thus to improve library, and by implication institutional, effectiveness and efficiency in relation to academic support;
4. to help the library demonstrate its effectiveness and value to the University at large;

5. thus to help the University demonstrate its sense of responsibility to society.

It is to be hoped that in such reviews there will be attempts to isolate the separate contributions of the library to the support of research as opposed to teaching and learning.

USER INVOLVEMENT AND FEEDBACK

The development of citizens' charters, and various off-shoots such as student charters, has emphasized the need for services of all kinds to state what they are doing and provide some means of feedback. No library exists in isolation from its users, who may have very direct involvement with funding (see Figure 10.1).

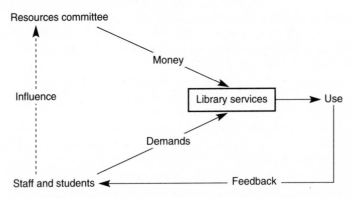

Figure 10.1. The academic library and its environment.

In the past many surveys of users were undertaken at the drop of a hat by librarians who had the feeling they had problems and were not certain how to solve them. As indicated in Chapter 9, the literature on user studies is littered with exhortations (Powell, 1988) to build on previous work and lamentations that comparatively few surveys of users are ever reported as having led to modifications, let alone improvements, in services. Such a position is no longer tenable. It is clear that services such as libraries are well advised to conduct surveys of users and to draw on similar evidence from other sources which contribute to providing user feedback. In educational institutions the use of feedback from students on courses is almost universal, and increasingly such feedback refers to library services. This is a natural outcome of wider surveys of students' opinions which show the importance of library facilities. For example, a report published by the Quality in Higher Education Project (Barnett, 1994) identified 111 criteria of quality common to the groups surveyed. Three out of the five most highly rated criteria are directly concerned with library provision. These are:

- that there is adequate access to library facilities (time and location);
- that the library has adequate resources to cater for the learning demands of students;
- that the library has adequate resources to cater for the teaching demands of staff.

The high value placed on libraries by students ensures that the nature and adequacy of feedback mechanisms will be the subject of enquiry by quality assurance teams.

A common approach is to conduct a user survey structured to obtain an assessment of the importance and the quality of the service on the occasion of the survey. These surveys can operate at a variety of levels, from the top level ('how good was the library service today?'), through more specific aspects ('were you satisfied with the attitude of the staff?'), to a measurement of the outcome of library service delivery ('did this book do for you what you hoped it would do?').

INFORMATION TECHNOLOGY AND MANAGEMENT INFORMATION

When library procedures were first automated in the late 1960s a number of forward thinking librarians preached the cause of management information. This was seen as an essential component of the planning and evaluation cycle, as indeed it is, and the power of the computer as a godsend. The difficulty at that time was that, first, there were few librarians in practice who grasped the full concepts of the planning and evaluation cycle and, second, the other audiences or partners at the institutional level were often less interested in these concepts. For this reason management information was not always built into automated library systems in the most helpful manner, and has sometimes had to be bolted on in an awkward fashion. As the real value of resources devoted to library services has

declined, so planning and evaluation has become much more important to all partners. There are two approaches to remedying the
deficiencies in management information systems. The first way, pio-
neered at De Montfort University, has been to develop a decision
support system based on PC software which can take data from a
variety of sources and synthesize them to assist managers in decision making. The second approach, exemplified by research based at
De Montfort University and elsewhere, is to prescribe the performance indicators, and hence the statistical measures and management information, which are needed to evaluate the effectiveness of
the library service. The data elements defined by this prescription
are then effectively the minimum requirements for the management
information outputs of future automated systems.

The rapid development of electronic information sources and services cannot be ignored in a chapter that looks forward. A
noticeable trend is that publishers and database compilers are
increasingly targeting end-users, not just to promote the searching
of databases online, but also to sell the kind of document delivery
services alluded to in Chapter 5. The undoubted added value of
these services has to be assessed against their added costs, and
such assessment may be difficult in highly devolved budgetary systems such as those becoming common in universities. With such
arrangements it is possible to make suboptimal decisions. For
example, a teaching department might pay for the electronic delivery of documents identified in a database search, even though
copies of the documents in printed form are housed in the university library. The library, which has a primary role in information
provision, needs to take a positive role within the university in
defining the limits and loci of responsibility. The existence of a
framework for the systematic evaluation of services will clearly
assist the library in registering its interest and promoting its role
in this regard.

Another aspect which needs to be considered is organizational.
The trend towards the convergence of libraries and computing services is likely to continue, although this is unlikely to lead to a
merger in all institutions (Lovecy, 1994). The pressures leading to
convergence include the increased use of information technology in
libraries, the reliance of libraries on networks, the activities of the
Combined Higher Education Software Team (CHEST), and the
demand for information strategies. Where there is a merger, the
combined service will clearly be evaluated in a uniform way; and

even where there is no merger, but coordination, common systems of evaluation are desirable.

THE QUEST FOR STANDARDS

The differences in perspective between different bodies with an interest in evaluation have to be borne in mind when devising any system for continuous assessment. Table 10.1 is an updated version of a matrix of evaluation which first appeared several years ago, showing the primary perspective of the various participants in the evaluation process.

Table 10.1 Perspectives on evaluation

Target audiences → Frames of reference ↓	Library users	Library managers	Library funders	Gov't agencies e.g. HEFCs	Librarians' professional bodies, e.g. SCONUL, LA	Other professional bodies, e.g. SPTL, Engineering Council
User needs	X	X			X	X
Money cost		X	X	X		
Published standards		X			X	X
Other libraries	X	X	X	X		X
Other information agencies	X	X		X		X
Librarians' professional expectations		X			X	
Peer group		X				

Funding agencies and governments both have an interest in comparing the performances of organizations which appear to be similar in nature. Library managers share this interest to a certain extent although they are always quick to point out the differences, however insignificant, between their own organization and a superficially similar one. Clearly a standardization of methods, definitions and terminology can help in the making of comparisons. Another pressure towards standardization comes from managers themselves who may not have a background in, or an understanding of, the principles of measurement and evaluation sufficient to determine an approach from first principles. It is at these two audiences that standards are aimed.

Standardization operates at three levels. There is the basic level of data collection; there is the level at which performance indicators are defined; and there is the integrative level, that is the framework within which evaluation is undertaken or performance assessed. It is rare to find a single published work in which all three levels are to be found.

There are now in progress a number of initiatives, about to come to fruition, which will have an impact on performance assessment in academic libraries.

International

At the international level there are three organizations concerned with standardization. International Federation of Library Associations (IFLA), through its University Libraries Section, is producing a manual of performance indicators specifically for academic libraries (IFLA, 1993). This includes definitions of performance indicators, and some details of methods of data collection. The International Standards Organisation (ISO) is proposing a standard which will define a number of performance indicators which are either widely used or have been well tested and can be safely recommended to a wide audience, even though some of the indicators will not have universal application. The standard includes a limited amount of information on methods of data collection. Finally, in the interests of cross-border comparisons, the European Commission has funded a number of projects in this general area. The first project, based at De Montfort University, the Library and Information Statistics Unit and Essex County Library, has built on earlier work on decision support systems (Adams 1993) to develop a 'toolbox' of library performance indicators: a set of definitions of indicators and attributes to which they are related. This list of performance indicators forms the basis of further work which will bring together librarians and suppliers of library automation systems to produce decision support systems. Library automation systems suppliers will be encouraged to ensure that the management information generated from their systems at the very least conforms with the definitions of the toolbox. The outcomes of these initiatives are likely to be influential in terms of defining indicators and data elements.

National

At the national level initiatives come from two directions. In the United States the American Library Association, a professional body, has produced practical manuals, including that of Van House *et al.* (1990) explored in Chapter 1. This influential publication defines a number of performance indicators and not only sets out in detail methods of collecting data but makes suggestions as to how the indicators can be presented and used to evaluate performance. In the United Kingdom there has been no comparable production – indeed, one is not necessary; but there has been a report referred to in Chapter 4, which not only defines performance indicators (specifically for FE colleges), but also sets recommended levels for those indicators (Burness, 1993). In some ways this returns to a long-abandoned type of 'standard': the standard of provision, such as 'minimum funding = £20 per FTE student'. However, the report also recommends a range of indicators which, while not new in themselves, are designed to draw the attention of funding agencies and others to the possibilities of systematic evaluation.

As this book has shown, there is now a considerable literature which can enable almost any library manager to measure appropriate aspects of their service in ways which are appropriate to their own organization. Increasingly it has to be recognized, however, that the degree to which comparability can be demonstrated is limited. There are legitimate differences between organizations which have broadly similar objectives and the consensus view is that most organizations prefer to be assessed against their own specific objectives. One of the dangers with all comparisons and with the standardization of definition is that too much emphasis is placed on purely numerical measures. This has been recognized in the work undertaken by COPOL and SCONUL and taken up by the funding councils for higher education in the United Kingdom. The framework proposed for general use in British academic libraries recognizes that evaluation can be both objective and subjective, that numbers can be both cardinal and ordinal, and that some indicators of performance show the presence or absence of a facility or service rather than its scope, level of provision or degree of take-up by the users.

In general, measurement is not a problem. Once it has been determined what has to be measured then methods become fairly obvious. There are some exceptions to this rule, particularly where complete measurement is costly or intrusive, or where alternative measures give different results. In these cases it is helpful to have standardized methods and guidance which can be offered to less-knowledgeable practitioners on which methods to choose in the given circumstances. For example, however desirable it may be to measure the amount of use made of documents in libraries, it is in practice extremely difficult, and there is a good case to be made for standardizing a relatively simple approach.

STAFF PARTICIPATION

Libraries have, in the main, operated with autocratic or hierarchical 'top-down' management styles. In a responsive, user-orientated, organization it is important to mobilize the full human resources in the interests of improving the service. Much of the most valuable feedback on the service is directed informally to staff in contact with the clients, and this will be lost if there are not adequate mechanisms for capturing it. If staff have an opportunity to contribute ideas and opinions as part of the decision-making process they are more likely to 'own' those decisions. The logical consequence is to move towards a more participative style of team management. Successful libraries, then, will operate with participative styles, but many staff have grown up with older styles, and may have difficulty adjusting to the new approach. The introduction of performance evaluation may help in facilitating such adjustment. The evaluation of performance is an essential part of management at all levels. Therefore it follows that, since everyone is at the very least the manager of their own time, everyone is involved in performance evaluation. The increasing realization of this elementary idea thus goes hand in hand with the spread of participative decision making.

PLANNING

The essential planning and evaluation cycle has not changed much, if at all, in the last 30 years. There have been many 'initiatives', often distinguished by sets of initials – MBO, PPBS, ZBBS, MRAP, PBB, TQM – all of which seem to have been like passing fancies and all essentially the same. All reduce in their essentials to the cycle shown in Figure 10.2.

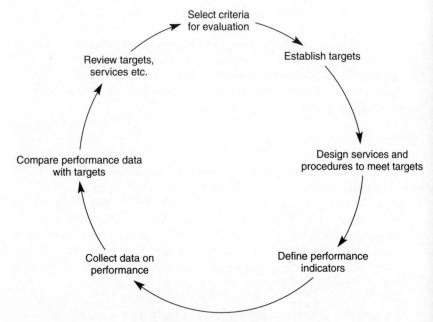

Figure 10.2. The planning cycle.

It is clearly desirable to devise an approach to evaluation which will enable the library manager, who inevitably will have to collect the data, to assess performance for his or her own purposes, for institutions' internal reviews, and for external reviews in a consistent fashion. The approach will also have to accommodate all the trends discussed so far in this chapter. In the chosen evaluation system:

- procedures must be explicit;
- definitions must be precise;
- performance indicators must allow for differences in purpose, clientele and size of libraries;
- both users and library staff must be involved;
- new developments in electronic information service delivery must be accommodated;

- national and international standards for defining statistical measures and performance indicators must be accommodated;
- other services related organizationally to libraries must be accommodated;
- everything must be subject to audit.

THE SCONUL APPROACH

An example of a particular approach to performance assessment is an outcome of the Follett report on library provision in higher education (Joint Funding Councils' Libraries Review Group, 1993) which recommended the development of a framework for evaluation. This framework is based on earlier work undertaken by members of COPOL and SCONUL (SCONUL, 1992) and now proposed by the funding councils (Joint Funding Councils, 1995). It provides five criteria which can be generalized to provide a framework for the evaluation of any library and information service. There are two dimensions to the framework: the criteria themselves, and the activities undertaken by or in the library.

Criteria for Evaluation

Integration
This assesses the degree to which the library's objectives are integrated with the objectives of the funding body. How does the library contribute to the teaching, learning and research objectives of the institution? Here it will be necessary to show how the library service is integrated with the institution's planning and review system, to describe the mechanisms for capturing and reporting feedback, and to demonstrate that those mechanisms are used. SCONUL is developing a manual, based on the COPMED document (Committee of Postgraduate Medical Deans), for use in the accreditation of libraries. Parts of this manual provide guidelines on this aspect of evaluation. Evaluation using this criterion might be demonstrated through the answers to questions such as:

- Does the university have an information strategy?
- Does the library have written objectives prepared in collaboration with representatives of the academic and user community?
- Does the library offer services to all personnel within the institution?

- Is there a formalized process of regular consultation with the academic and user community?

User Satisfaction

This criterion is used to assess the evidence that the library satisfies the customers or users of the service. All these sources have been discussed in previous chapters, but it is helpful to bring them together now to reinforce their importance:

- users' committees, panels, liaison/discussion/focus groups;
- suggestions books/boxes (and electronic equivalents);
- course monitoring and evaluation;
- academic committees;
- user surveys;
- informal contact with users.

SCONUL will provide guidance on surveying users, and model survey instruments in five areas:

- enquiry services (Chapter 7);
- availability of materials (Chapter 5);
- evaluation of stock (Chapter 5);
- quality of service (Chapters 5–7);
- general satisfaction (Chapters 4–7).

The documentation accompanying these survey instruments will enable libraries to incorporate these measurement techniques in local evaluation of library services without specialist training or advice.

Service Delivery

There are two aspects to this criterion: at the more judgemental or subjective end, there is the assessment of the degree to which the service meets targets for delivery; at the more quantitative or objective end, there are numbers describing the use made of the service. The performance indicators will be judgements about locally determined objectives, while others will be nationally monitored quantitative measures. The locally developed targets will be of two kinds. The first of these relates to developments in service, for example the installation of a cluster of computers for public use. The other kind of target relates to service standards, for example the acquisition of a book which the library does not have within three weeks for a student.

Efficiency

There are a number of ways of defining efficiency. At the baseline it is a measure of the cheapness with which services are delivered sufficiently to meet objectives. It gives a measure of value for money; it is a way of saying, given the level of resources available is the level of outputs high or low? Libraries are very complex organizations, with many different outputs, and the outputs of some activities form the inputs to others. When looking at efficiency it is important that identifiable costs and resources are used. The average cost of a loan should not be defined as

$$\frac{\text{Total number of loans}}{\text{Total library expenditure}}$$

but rather as

$$\frac{\text{Total number of loans}}{\text{Expenditure on loans service}}$$

Admittedly, the latter is more difficult to calculate precisely. It is at this point that managers need to ask themselves about the degree of precision needed in the answer.

Economy

Indicators of economy reflect the relationship between resources and costs on the one hand and the target population on the other. This is one of the most traditional ways of evaluating the effectiveness of the service. The indicators of economy, such as 'Total library expenditure per FTE student' have in fact given evaluation a bad name because they have often been used in isolation. The value of putting these indicators into a framework enables evaluators to see them in a wider context.

Library Activities

The second dimension of the framework enumerates the activities undertaken by or within the library. There are a number of ways of categorizing these activities, many of which are valid. It is important that the framework both incorporates all existing activities, so that library staff can see their own positions, and can accommodate additional services. The SCONUL category groups are listed in Appendix VI.

Using the Framework

Table 10.2 Summary of the SCONUL framework.

Components	How measured	Categories and definitions	Examples	Scale example
Statistical measures	Objective, absolute	Population	FTEs	4981
"	"	Costs	Binding	£12,357
"	"	Resources	Space	15,000m^2
"	"	"	Staff	13 LAs
"	"	"	Serials received	2314
"	"	Use	Items lent	235,921
Indicators				
Economy	Objective, absolute	Costs: population	Total spend per FTE	£299.32
"	"	Resources: population	Seat-hours per week per FTE	11.2
Efficiency	Objective, absolute	Costs: resources	Average staff cost	£13,201
"	"	Costs: use	Cost per loan	£0.51
"	"	Use: resources	Seat occupancy	35%
"	"	Use: population	Loans per FTE	45.32
Service delivery	Relative to targets	Development targets	Almost any	
"	Objective	Service standards	Speed of processing	3 months
"	"	"	Accuracy of answers to enquiries	65%
User satisfaction	Subjective	Satisfaction	%age of users satisfied	63%
Integration	Mainly subjective, Some objective		Course feedback available to library?	Yes

Table 10.3 Suggested performance indicators.

Activity	Service delivery	Efficiency	Economy
Provision of collections	Volumes per FTE student	Items processed per FTE member of library staff Cost per item added	Expenditure per FTE student on acquisition of information
Public services	Documents delivered per FTE student	Documents delivered per FTE member of library staff Staff cost per document delivered	
Information services	Proportion of students receiving post-induction instruction in information handling skills Enquiries answered per FTE student	Enquiries answered per FTE member of professional library staff Staff cost per enquiry	FTE students per FTE member of professional library staff
Study facilities	Library study hours per FTE student	Percentage seat occupancy	FTE students per seat
Whole service			FTE students per library Total library space per FTE student Library staff expenditure and operating costs per FTE student Total library expenditure per FTE student

Within this framework a number of indicators have been proposed, which are designed to give a balanced picture of library services. None of the indicators should be used in isolation, since all aspects are interrelated. The indicators should be used within a review process, and should reflect locally determined objectives. The more detailed indicators should be used only within a library, but should still be related to the overall framework. The framework meets the requirements set out in the Planning section above, and can be used in a number of contexts, for example funding council teaching quality assessments, Higher Education Quality Council quality audits, local planning and review processes, and day to day management of libraries

Table 10.2 summarizes the characteristics of the criteria and performance indicators, and Table 10.3 lists some indicators recommended for general use. Some of these will be published nationally.

Since the criteria are universal in their application, and the list of activities can accommodate further additions, it should be possible to use the SCONUL approach in the evaluation of other academic services. As stated, the concepts are suitable for application at a number of levels. It is particularly important at the micro-level to evaluate the developing electronic systems which add value or directly replace other formats, and the framework allows judgements on cost-effectiveness to be made in a systematic way.

Table 10.4 Evaluation of information system performance.

Criterion	Performance indicator
Integration	Subject coverage relative to institutional interests
User satisfaction	Percentage of users satisfied with retrieved documents
Service delivery	Percentage of retrieved documents delivered within given time period
Efficiency	Cost per search Number of searches per head of population Percentage of retrieved documents actually read
Economy	Cost per head of population

It is appropriate to round off this chapter with an example of the use of the SCONUL approach in the evaluation of one of the electronic services now widely available for searching by end users, who are often comparatively unsophisticated in developing search strategies. The performance indicators that could be used to assess each criterion are shown in Table 10.4.

Consideration of all aspects in the evaluation and the search for appropriate indicators might lead to a reawakening of interest in such measures as precision, relevance, pertinence, and threshold of interest (Cleverdon, 1990).

In conclusion, there is no doubt that more formal methods of evaluation and assessment of libraries and information services will become more important. Methods may become more sophisticated but the essentials will remain the same. The climate is now one in which assessment is the norm, not just for enthusiastic librarians but for all the partners in educational services, whether they be users, professionals delivering services, managers, funding authorities or governments.

Appendix I: Survey questionnaire: further education libraries

LIBRARY SERVICES – FURTHER EDUCATION SECTOR

Name of institution ....

Please tick as appropriate

QUESTION 1: WRITTEN COMMITMENT TO PERFORMANCE ASSESSMENT

Does your institution have a written commitment to assessing the performance of the library service?

YES ☐   NO ☐

QUESTION 2: LIBRARY POLICY ON PERFORMANCE ASSESSMENT

Does the library have a written policy on performance assessment of the library service?

YES ☐   NO ☐

QUESTION 3: READER SERVICES

Has the library evaluated any of the following services during the last 12 months?

Service		Methods used
Book/periodical usage	☐	....
Book/periodical availability	☐	....
Reservations (turnaround time)	☐	....
Interlibrary loans (turnaround time)	☐	....
Readers' enquiry service	☐	....
User education/library skills	☐	....
Other reader services	☐	....

....

....

QUESTION 4: FEEDBACK FROM USERS

In what ways does your library seek feedback from users on the library service generally?

Course monitoring/evaluation ☐
Formal discussion groups ☐
Satisfaction surveys ☐
Informal discussion ☐
Other .... ☐

....

QUESTION 5: SATISFACTION WITH CURRENT PROCEDURES

How satisfied are you with current procedures for assessing the library's performance?

Very satisfied ☐   Satisfied ☐   Not very satisfied ☐   Dissatisfied ☐

QUESTION 6: GENERAL COMMENTS

Do you have any other general comments to make about assessment of library services – either in your own library or within FE libraries generally?

....

....

....

....

....

....

....

I would like to thank you for taking the time to complete this questionnaire.

Steve Morgan

Appendix II: Survey questionnaire: higher education libraries

Name of institution ....

Please tick as appropriate

QUESTION 1: WRITTEN COMMITMENT TO PERFORMANCE ASSESSMENT

Does your institution have a written commitment to assessing the performance of the library service?

YES ☐   NO ☐

If YES, is it written in

the institution's mission statement? ☐

Other (please specify) ....

I would be grateful if you could return (along with this questionnaire) a copy of a mission statement if it includes information on performance assessment

QUESTION 2: LIBRARY POLICY ON PERFORMANCE ASSESSMENT

Does the library have a written policy on performance assessment of the library service?

YES ☐   NO ☐

If YES, is performance assessment

  (a) contained in one discrete policy? ☐

  (b) covered in a range of library policies on different topics? ☐

If NO, could you give your reasons?:-

....

....

....

QUESTION 3: THREE SERVICES TO LIBRARY USERS

Below are questions concerning assessment of THREE categories of service to library users. Even if the assessment has taken place at only ONE of your site libraries, please fill in as appropriate.

(a) DOCUMENT DELIVERY SERVICES

Has your library carried out any evaluation of book/periodical collections during the last 12 months?

YES ☐   NO ☐

If YES, please tick and give brief details   methods employed

1. BOOK COLLECTIONS
2. PERIODICALS COLLECTIONS
3. INTER LIBRARY LOANS SERVICE
4. RESERVATIONS SERVICE

If NO, could you give your reasons?:-

....

....

....

(b) READERS' ENQUIRY SERVICE

Has the performance of the Readers' Enquiry Service been evaluated during the last 12 months?

YES ☐   NO ☐

If YES, which of these evaluation methods were used?

Interviews ☐   Course board/committee ☐
Survey
Observation ☐   Other (please specify) ....

If YES, which of these groups were consulted?

Students ☐   Library staff ☐
Academic staff ☐
                    Other (please specify) ....

If NO, could you give your reasons?:-

....

....

....

(c) USER EDUCATION (inc. ORIENTATION OR
    BIBLIOGRAPHICAL INSTRUCTION)

Has the performance of your user education been evaluated during the last
12 months?

YES [   ]   NO [   ]

If YES, which of these evaluation methods were used?

Interviews   [   ]   Course board/committee [   ]
Survey
Observation   [   ]   Other (please specify) ....

If YES, which of these groups were consulted?

Students   [   ]   Library staff [   ]
Academic staff [   ]
                             Other (please specify) ....

If NO, could you give your reasons?:- ....
....
....

QUESTION 4: OTHER READER SERVICES

Has the performance of any other services to library users been evaluated
during the last 12 months?

YES [   ]   NO [   ]

If YES, which services have been evaluated?

....
....

QUESTION 5: PERFORMANCE ASSESSMENT RESULTS

Have the results of any library performance assessment been disseminated
outside of the library during the last 12 months?

YES [   ]   NO [   ]

If YES, which of the following bodies have received them?

Academic staff   [   ]   Library committee [   ]
Course boards/committees   [   ]   Students   [   ]
Management of institution/ [   ]
  governors   Other (please specify) ....

If NO, could you give your reasons?:-

....
....

QUESTION 6: SATISFACTION WITH CURRENT PROCEDURES

How satisfied are you with current procedures for assessing your library's performance? Please tick on the scale as appropriate.

Very Satisfied   Totally Dissatisfied

10	9	8	7	6	5	4	3	2	1

QUESTION 7: IMPROVEMENT OF PROCEDURES

Are there any ways in which you think your libary's performance assessment procedures could be improved?

YES [   ]   NO [   ]

If YES, please give brief details:

....

....

....

....

QUESTION 8: GENERAL COMMENTS

Do you have any other general comments to make about the assessment of your library's performance?

....

....

....

....

I would like to thank you for taking the time to complete this questionnaire.

Appendix III: Materials availability survey

Form 5–1
Materials Availability Survey

DID YOU FIND IT?

PLEASE HELP US IMPROVE SERVICE by telling us whether you found the library materials you looked for today. Use this form as scratch paper while you look in the catalog and on the shelf.

Your status (check one)

_____ 1. Undergraduate   _____ 4. Research staff
_____ 2. Graduate student   _____ 5. Other staff
_____ 3. Faculty   _____ 6. Other (what?) _____

If you were NOT looking for library materials today, please check here ____ and stop. THANK YOU!

Author/Title/Journal/etc. (abbreviations are fine)	Call#	Found on shelf? CIRCLE	
_____		Yes	No
_____		Yes	No
_____		Yes	No
_____		Yes	No
_____		Yes	No

OVERALL, how <u>successful</u> were you at finding materials today?

      1   2   3   4   5
Not at all   Completely successful

What will you use these materials for? Primarily:

_____ 1. Course work   _____ 4. Current awareness
_____ 2. Research   _____ 5. A mix of several purposes
_____ 3. Teaching   _____ 6. Other: _____

MORE ITEMS? COMMENTS? Use the back of this form. THANK YOU!

PLEASE DROP IN BOX AT EXIT AS YOU LEAVE.

Appendix IV: Reference services statistics

Form 13–1
Reference Services Statistics
Daily Desk Reporting Form

Name: _____   Date: _____
May be a department, unit, or individual (as appropriate)

Hour	Reference	Total
8–9		
9–11		
11–1		
1–3		
3–5		
5–7		
7–9		
9–		

Total: _____

Appendix V: Reference satisfaction survey

Form 14–1
Reference Satisfaction Survey

PLEASE LET US KNOW HOW WE ARE DOING. Evaluate the *reference* service that you received today by circling one number on each of the following scales. Feel free to explain – use the back of the form.

If you were NOT asking a reference question today, please check here _____ and stop. Thank you.

1. *Relevance* of information provided:

   Not relevant   1   2   3 . 4   5   Very relevant

2. Satisfaction with the *amount* of information provided:

   Not satisfied 1   2   3   4   5   Very satisfied
   (too little, too much)   (the right amount)

3. *Completeness* of the answer that you received:

   Not complete 1   2   3   4   5   Very complete

4. *Helpfulness* of staff:

   Not helpful   1   2   3   4   5   Extraordinarily helpful

5. Overall, how *satisfied* are you?:

   Not satisfied 1   2   3   4   5   Extremely satisfied

Why? _____

_____

6. You are:

   _____ 1. Undergraduate   _____ 4. Research staff
   _____ 2. Graduate student   _____ 5. Other staff
   _____ 3. Faculty   _____ 6. Other? _____

7. What will you use this information for?

   _____ 1. Course work   _____ 4. Mix of several purposes
   _____ 2. Research   _____ 5. Current awareness
   _____ 3. Teaching   _____ 6. Other? _____

THANK YOU! Please leave this questionnaire in the box.

USE BACK OF PAGE FOR ANY ADDITIONAL COMMENTS.

Appendix VI: Follett Report
(Annex C): performance indicators

ANNEX C

Performance Indicators

Proposed Framework

1. Framework discussed in Chapter 10 could be developed based on the following principles which are largely taken from work carried out by SCONUL and COPOL.

   a. *Integration* – how far library objectives are linked to institutional objectives. Particular factors would be: what evidence is there to show the effective integration of the library service into the teaching, learning and research planning and review system, so that feedback is transmitted between departments and the library in both directions? does actual feedback occur in planning and delivery? This will largely be a judgemental, rather than a numerical indicator. Some relevant indicators however – such as the scale of borrowing by users – can contain numerical elements.

   b. *User satisfaction* – what evidence is there to show that users are satisfied with library support for their courses and research, in particular in relation to the supply of book, periodical and other media, study facilities, and information services and information skills tuition?

   c. *Effectiveness* – this relates outputs to service targets. These can be output measures and service standards. They could cover availability of materials, the time taken to process new accessions, reservations and recalls, interlibrary loans, appropriateness of output (e.g. enquiry responses). Although there can be numerical components for this (e.g.

documents supplied per FTE), it would be possible to aggregate them in a non0numeric measure. The assessment of information support for researchers depends critically on this indicator, and this would have to be more judgemental, since targets are more difficult to establish numerically.

d. *Efficiency and value for money* – this links inputs to outputs to indicate value for money. The essentialy question is: taking account of the level of input, is the quantity and range of output high? Such measures could include loans, number of enquiries, photocopying volume, all in relation to costs. Wherever possible, identified costs should be used, with total costs only being used as a backstop. Libraries have multiple outputs, which raises the problem of using one as a proxy or trying to add different kinds of outputs.

e. *Economy* – this relates inputs to clientele, such as overall library costs per FTE staff and/or operating costs per FTE student, or per academic staff, etc. A similar ratio for acquisitions or information inputs can also give an indication of comparative levels of provision. These are numeric measures, but the significance of high or low figures may vary for different types of institution. Essentially this figure should be seen as a control against the others: the framework allows this concept to be placed in context. It is also critically important that the indicators used are consistent and accurate with no variation of definition across all institutions considered.

2. It should be noted that the framework is not meant to imply that particular indicators are better than others. The framework allows institutions to choose appropriate indicators for their circumstances and to decide what is good or bad in that context.

Activity Groupings

3. Performance indicators require not only a common set of statistics, but also some grouping of library activities. These may differ between institutions because of their different activities and aims, but they may be grouped together for performance indicator purposes. They might include:

a. *Provision of stock* – acquisitions, cataloguing and classification.

b. *Public services* – circulation, shelving, ILL, photocopying, electronic document delivery.

    c. *Information services* – Enquiry desk, information retrieval mediated by library staff, user education.

    d. *Study facilities* – study places, audio-visual and other facilities.

    e. *Other facilities* – binding and conservation, special collections, photographic and media services.

    f. *Management activities* – Policy making, liaison with users, staff management, staff development, promotion of library services.

External Presentation

4. The combination of numeric and nonnumeric indicators presents difficulties. At the highest level, a 5-point scale (Outstanding, Good, Satisfactory, Shortcomings, and Poor) could be adopted to give an overall indicator of performance.

5. At the more detailed levels, a small number of indicators would be regularly presented (some annually, others at slightly longer intervals) using some standard indicators, such as the proportion of institutional expenditure devoted to the library, but primarily using the framework described above. In order to provide a common framework for user input, the user satisfaction survey outlined by Van House *et al.* (1990), could be adopted (suitably amended if necessary). This could not be undertaken annual, but might be carried out at longer intervals. Individual institutions might also with to add specific indicators relating to their own circumstances: a library with space problems might, for example, usefully add indicators relating to occupied and empty shelving, or occupancy data.

Internal Library Management

6. Indicators could be used by different staff at a number of levels. These would make the fullest use of a matrix of the principles and the activities/ groupings above. The specific indicators used would vary to accommodate the needs of the individual institutions. There could be a significantly higher number of indicators for internal purposes than for external presentation. The framework, however, remains constant, so that the smaller group of indicators can be seen in the context of the larger, and can be produced if required.

References and further reading

Abbott, C. (1994) *Performance Measurement in Library and Information Services*. London: Aslib.

Adams, M. and McElroy, R. (1994) *Colleges, Libraries and Access to Learning*. London: Library Association Publishing.

Adams, R. (1993) *Decision Support Systems and Performance Assessment in Academic Libraries*. London: Bowker Saur.

Advisory, Conciliation and Arbitration Service (1988) *Employee Appraisal*. (Advisory Booklet No.11) London: ACAS.

Albrecht, K. (1992) *At America's Service: How Your Company Can Join the Customer Service Revolution*. New York: Warner.

Anderson, G. C. (1993) *Managing Performance Appraisal Systems*. Oxford: Blackwell.

Association of College and Research Libraries (1983) *Evaluating Bibliographic Instruction: a Handbook*. Chicago: American Library Association.

Auckland, M. (1990) 'Training for staff appraisal.' In Prytherch, R. (ed.) *Handbook of Library Training Practice*, Vol.2. Aldershot: Gower, pp.90–112.

Barker, L. and Enright, S. (1993) 'Academic related staff appraisal at Imperial College Libraries: a peer review scheme.' *British Journal of Academic Librarianship* **8** (2), 113–128.

Baker, S. L. and Lancaster, F. W. (1991) *The Measurement and Evaluation of Library Services* (2nd ed.). Arlington, Va.: Information Resources Press.

Barnett, R. (1994) *Assessment of the Quality of Higher Education: a Review and an Evaluation*. London: University of London Institute of Education Centre for Higher Education Studies.

Bawden, D. (1990) *User-Oriented Evaluation of Information Systems and Services*. Aldershot: Gower.

Beed, T. W. and Stimpson, R. J. (1985) *Survey Interviewing*. London: Unwin Hyman.

Benson, J. (1980) 'Bibliographic education: a radical assessment.' In Oberman-Soroka, C. (ed.) *Proceedings from the Second Southeastern Conference on Approaches to Bibliographic Instruction, 22–23 March, 1979.* Charleston, S.C.: College of Charleston. pp.53–68.

Berkner, D. (1983) 'Library staff development through performance appraisal.' In Person, R. (1983) *The Management Process: a Selection of Readings for Librarians.* Chicago: American Library Association, pp.327–341.

Bibby, J., Eastwood, R. and Wisher, S. (1994) *College Libraries: a Case for Investment?* London: Library Association Publishing.

Billing, D. (ed.) (1980) *Indicators of Performance*: Papers presented at the 15th Annual Conference of the Society for Research into Higher Education, 1979. Guildford: Society for Research into Higher Education.

Blagden, J. (1988) 'Some thoughts on use and users.' *Iatul Quarterly* **2** (3), 125–134.

Blagden, J. and Harrington, J. (1990) *How Good is Your Library? A Review of Approaches to the Evaluation of Library and Information Services.* London: Aslib.

Blaikie, N. (1993) *Approaches to Social Enquiry.* Cambridge: Polity Press.

Blandy, S. G., Martin, L. M., and Strife, M. L. (eds.) (1992) 'Assessment and accountability in reference work.' *Reference Librarian* **38** (17) special issue.

Bluck, R., Hilton, A. and, Noon, P. (1994) *Information Skills in Academic Libraries: a Teaching and Learning Role in Higher Education.* (SEDA Paper No.82) Birmingham: Staff and Educational Development Association.

Bookstein, A. (1982) 'Sources of error in library questionnaires.' *Library Research* **4**, 85–94.

Booth, C. (1993) 'Quality: the national view.' In McElroy, A. R. (ed.) *Quality Matters: Proceedings of the Annual COFHE Study Conference University of Kent, Canterbury, 13–16 April 1992.* London: Library Association: COFHE. pp.7–10.

Bovaird, T., Gregory, D. and Martin, S. (1988) 'Performance measurement in urban economic development.' *Public Money and Management* **8** (4), 17–22.

Brember, V. L. and Leggate, P. (1985) 'Linking a medical user survey to management for library effectiveness 1. the user survey.' *Journal of Documentation* **41** (1), 1–14.

Brill, M. (1994) 'The cheating art.' *Sunday Times (Style and Travel),* 5 June. p.15.

Britten, W. A. (1990) 'A use statistic for collection management: the 80/20 rule revisited.' *Library Acquisitions: Practice and Theory* **14**, 183–189.

Brophy, P. (1989) 'Performance measurement in academic libraries: a

Polytechnic perspective. *British Journal of Academic Librarianship* **4** (2), 99–110.

Brophy, P., Coulling, K. and Melling, M. (1993) 'Quality management: a university approach.' *Aslib Information* **21** (6), 246–248.

Buckland, M. K. (1975) *Book Availability and the Library User*. New York: Pergamon Press.

Buckland, M. K. (1982) 'Concepts of library goodness.' *Canadian Library Journal* **39** (2), 63–66.

Bunge, C. A. (1985) 'Factors related to reference question answering success: the development of a data gathering form.' *RQ* **24** (4), 482–486.

Burness, T. J. (1993) *Libraries in Scottish FE Colleges: Standards for Performance and Resourcing*. Glasgow and Motherwell: Scottish Library and Information Council and Scottish Library Association.

Burr, R. L. (1979) 'Evaluating library collections: a case study.' *Journal of Academic Librarianship* **5** (5), 256–260.

Burton, P. (1990) 'Accuracy of information provision: the need for client-centred service.' *Journal of Librarianship* **22** (4), 201–215.

Busha, C. H. and Harter, S. P. (1980) *Research Methods in Librarianship: Techniques and Interpretation*. New York: Academic Press.

Butler, M. and Davis, H. (1992) 'Strategic planning as a catalyst for change in the 1990s.' *College and Research Libraries* **53** (5), 393–403.

Carpmael, C., Morgan, S. and Nichols, J. (1991) 'Library orientation: a workable alternative?' *Library Review* **41** (4), 16–30.

Carter, N. (1989) 'Performance indicators: 'backseat driving' or 'hands off' control?' *Policy and Politics* **17** (2), 131–138.

Casteleyn, M. and Webb, S. P. (1993) *Promoting Excellence: Personnel Management and Staff Development in Libraries*. London: Bowker Saur.

Cave, M., Hannay, S., Kogan, M. and Trevett, G. (1988) *The Use of Performance Indicators in Higher Education*. London: J. Kingsley.

Centre for Interfirm Comparison (1984) *Interlibrary Comparisons in Academic Libraries*. (BLR&D Report No.5763). London: British Library.

Childers, T. (1987) 'The quality of reference: still moot after 20 years.' *Journal of Academic Librarianship* **13** (2), 73–74.

Clapp, V. W. and Jordan, R. T. (1965) Quantitative criteria for adequacy of academic library collections. *College and Research Libraries* **26**, 371–380.

Cleverdon, C. (1990) Questions of relevance. In Bawden, D., *User-Oriented Evaluation of Information Systems and Services*. Aldershot: Gower. pp.165–171.

Cohen, L. R. (1989) 'Conducting performance evaluations.' *Library Trends* **38** (1), 40–52.

Committee of Postgraduate Medical Deans (1993) *Accreditation of*

Libraries in Support of Postgraduate Medical and Dental Education. London: National Health Service Regional Librarians' Group.

Cook, S. (1992) *Customer Care: Implementing Total Quality in Today's Service-Driven Organisation.* London: Kogan Page.

Corrall, S. M. (1993) 'The access model: managing the transformation at Aston University.' *Interlending and Document Supply* 21 (4), 13–23.

Corrall, S. M. (1994) *Strategic Planning for Library and Information Services.* London: Aslib.

Cotta-Schonberg, M. and Line, M. (1994) 'Evaluation of academic libraries: with special reference to the Copenhagen Business School Library.' *Journal of Librarianship and Information Science* 26 (2), 55–69.

Council for Further and Higher Education (1992) *Guidelines to Guidelines.* London: Library Association: COFHE Group.

Cowley, J. (1988) *A Survey of Information Skills Teaching in UK Higher Education* (British Library Research Paper No.47). London: British Library.

Cowley, J. and Hammond, N. (1987) *Educating Information Users in Universities, Polytechnics and Colleges* (British Library Research Reviews No.12). London: British Library.

Cronin, B. (1982) 'Taking the measure of service.' *Aslib Proceedings* 34 (6/7), 273–294.

Crowley, T. (1985) 'Half-right reference: is it true?' *RQ* 25 (1), 59–68.

Dalton, G. (1988) 'Performance measurement matters when evaluating the effectiveness of reference services.' *Mousaion* 6 (2), 28–46.

Dalton, G. M. E. (1992) 'Quantitative approach to user satisfaction in reference service evaluation.' *South African Journal of Library and Information Science* 60, 89–103.

Davies, J. (1994) 'The FEFC(E) inspectorate, quality considerations and college libraries and learning resource centres.' *COFHE Bulletin* 72, 2–5.

Davinson, D. (1980) *Reference Service.* London: Clive Bingley.

Delamont, S. (1981) 'All too familiar? A decade of classroom research.' *Educational Analysis* 3 (1), 69–83.

De Silva, R. (1985) 'An evaluation strategy for library instruction by open learning.' *Education Libraries Bulletin* 28 (1), 15–25.

Dolphin, P. (1990) 'Evaluation of user education programmes.' In Fleming, H. (ed.) *User Education in Academic Libraries.* London: Library Association Publishing. pp.73–89.

Dolphin, P. (1994) 'Student-driven route taken at Thames Valley.' *Library Association Record* 95 (4), 204–205.

Dykeman, A. and King, B. (1983) 'Term paper analysis: a proposal for evaluating bibliographic instruction.' *Research Strategies* 1, 14–21.

Edwards, S. (1991) 'Effects of a self-paced workbook on students' skills and attitudes.' *Research Strategies* 9, 180–188.

Elias, A. W. (1992) *The National Federation of Abstracting and Information Services Yearbook of the Information Industry 1992.* Medford, N.J.: Learned Information.

Ellis, D. and Norton, B. (1993) *Implementing BS5750/ISO9000 in Libraries.* London: Aslib.

Elzy, C. A. and Lancaster, F. W. (1990) 'Looking at a collection in different ways: a comparison of methods of bibliographic checking.' *Collection Management* **12**, 1–10.

Elzy, C. A., Nourie, A., Lancaster, F. W. and Joseph, K. M. (1991) 'Evaluating reference services in a large academic library.' *College and Research Libraries* **52** (5), 454–465

Erlandson, D. A., Harris, E. L., Skipper, B. L. and Allen, S. D. (1993) *Doing Naturalistic Inquiry: a Guide to Methods.* London: Sage.

Evans, E., Borko, H., and Ferguson, P. (1972) 'Review of criteria used to measure library effectiveness.' *Bulletin of the Medical Library Association* **60** (1), 102–110.

Farnham, D. and Horton, S. (eds.) (1993) *Managing the New Public Services.* London: Macmillan.

Feagley, E. M. (1955) *A Library Orientation Test for College Freshmen.* New York: Teachers' College Press, Columbia University.

Feather, J. and Marriott, R. (1993) 'Uncharted territory: academic libraries and the growth in student numbers.' *Library Review* **42** (3), 20–30.

Feinberg, R. P. and King, C. (1992) 'Performance evaluation in bibliographic instruction workshop courses: assessing what students do as a measure of what they know.' *Reference Services Review* **20** (2), 75–80.

Fielden, J. (1993) *Supporting Expansion: a Report on Human Resource Management in Academic Libraries for the Joint Funding Councils' Libraries Review Group.* Bristol: HEFCE.

Fjallbrant, N. (1977) 'Evaluation in a user education programme.' *Journal of Librarianship* **9** (2) April, 83–95.

Fjallbrant, N. and Malley, I. (1984) *User Education in Libraries* (2nd ed.). London: Clive Bingley.

Fleming, H. (1986) 'User education in academic libraries in the UK.' *British Journal of Academic Librarianship* **1** (1), 18–40.

Fleming, H. (ed.) (1990) *User Education in Academic Libraries.* London: Library Association Publishing.

Fletcher, C. (1993) *Appraisal: Routes to Improved Performance.* London: Institute of Personnel Management.

Fletcher, C. and Williams, R. (1992) *Performance Appraisal and Career Development* (2nd ed.). Cheltenham: Stanley Thornes.

Fletcher, J. (ed.) (1985) *Reader Services in Polytechnic Libraries.* Aldershot: Gower.

Flynn, N. (1993) *Public Sector Management* (2nd ed.) Hemel Hempstead: Harvester Wheatsheaf.

Ford, G. (ed.) (1977) *User Studies: an Introductory Guide and Select Bibliography* (BLR&D Report No.5375). Sheffield: Centre for Research on User Studies.

Ford, G. (1989a) 'Approaches to performance measurement:some observations on principles and practice.' *British Journal of Academic Librarianship* 4 (2), 74–87.

Ford, G. (1989b) 'A perspective on performance measurement.' *International Journal of Information and Library Research* 1, 12–23.

Ford, G. (1990) *Review of Methods Employed in Determining the Use of Library Stock*. London: BNBRF.

Ford, G. and MacDougall, A. (1992) *Performance Assessment in Academic Libraries: Final Report on a Feasibility Study* (BLR&D Report No.6085). London: British Library.

Freedman, J. and Bantly, H. A. (1986) Techniques of program evaluation. In Clark, A. S. and Jones, K. F. (eds.) *Teaching Librarians to Teach*. Metuchen, N.J.: Scarecrow Press. pp.188–204.

Frick, E. (1990) 'Qualitative evaluation of user education programs: the best choice?' *Research Strategies* 8, 4–13.

Further Education Funding Council (1993) *Assessing Achievement* (Circulars 93/11 and 93/28). Coventry: FEFC.

Gibbs, S. (1986) 'Staff appraisal.' In Prytherch, R. (ed.) *Handbook of Library Training Practice*. Aldershot: Gower, pp.61–81.

Gibson, C. (1992) Accountability for bibliographic instruction programs in academic libraries: key issues for the 1990s. *Reference Librarian* 38, 99–108.

Goodall, D. L. (1988) 'Performance measurement: a historical perspective.' *Journal of Librarianship* 20 (2), 128–144.

Gorman, G. E. and Howes, B. R. (1989) *Collection Development for libraries*. London: Bowker Saur.

Green, A. (1993) 'A survey of staff appraisal in university libraries.' *British Journal of Academic Librarianship* 8 (3), 193–209.

Hafner, A. W. (1989) *Descriptive Statistical Techniques for Librarians*. Chicago: American Library Association.

Hamburg, M., Clelland, R. C., Bommer, M., Ramist, L. E. and Whitfield, R. M. (1974) *Library Planning and Decision-Making Systems*. Cambridge, Mass.: MIT Press.

Hanson, J. R. (1984) 'The evaluation of library user education with reference to the programme at Dorset Institute of Higher Education.' *Journal of Librarianship* 16 (1), 1–18.

Hardesty, L. (1981) 'Use of library materials at a small liberal arts college.' *Library Research* 3, 261–282.

Hardesty, L., Lovrich, N. P. and Manon, J. (1979) 'Evaluating library use instruction.' *College and Research Libraries* 40 (4), 309–317.

Hardesty, L., Schmitt, J. and Tucker, J. M. (1986) *User Instruction in*

Academic Libraries: a Century of Selected Readings. Metuchen, N.J.: Scarecrow Press.

Harris, C. (1977) 'Illuminative evaluation of user education programmes.' *Aslib Proceedings* **29** (10) Oct, 348–362.

Harris, M. (1991) 'The user survey in performance measurement.' *British Journal of Academic Librarianship* **6** (1), 1–12.

Harrison, C. (1989) 'Performance measures.' *COFHE Bulletin* **56**, 2–7.

Hatchard, D. B. and Toy, P. (1984) 'Evaluation of a library instruction program at BCAE.' *Australian Academic and Research Libraries* **15**, 157–167.

Heery, M. (1993) 'New model librarians: a question of realism.' *Journal of Librarianship and Information Science* **25** (3), 137–142.

Henry, G. T. (1990) *Practical Sampling*. London: Sage.

Henty, M (1989) 'Performance indicators in higher education libraries.' *British Journal of Academic Librarianship* **4** (3), 177–191.

Her Majesty's Stationery Office (1991) *Citizen's Charter: Raising the Standard*. London: HMSO.

Hernon, P. and McClure, C. R. (1987a) 'Where do we go from here? A final response. Contribution to the Continuing Debate on Library Reference Service:a mini symposium.' *Journal of Academic Librarianship* **13** (5), 282–284.

Hernon, P. and McClure, C. R. (1987b) *Unobtrusive Testing and Library Reference Services*. Norwood, N.J.: Ablex Publishing.

Hernon, P. and McClure, C. R. (1987c) 'Quality of data issues in unobtrusive testing of library reference service: recommendations and strategies.' *Library and Information Science Research* **9** (2), 77–93.

Higher Education Quality Council (1993) *University of Oxford: Quality Audit Report*. Birmingham: HEQC Division of Quality Audit.

Hindle, A. and Buckland, M. K. (1978) 'In-house book usage in relation to circulation.' *Collection Management* **2** (4), 265–277.

Horton, W. (1989) 'Interlibrary loan turnaround times in science and engineering.' *Special Libraries* **80**, 245–250.

IFLA (1993) *Measuring Quality: International Guidelines for Performance Measurement in Academic Libraries*. Munster: IFLA University Libraries and Other General Research Libraries Section. (Preliminary draft).

Isaac–Henry, K., Painter, C. and Barnes, C. (eds.) (1993) *Management in the Public sector*. London: Chapman and Hall.

Jackson, P. (1988) 'The management of performance in the public sector.' *Public Money and Management* **8** (4), 11–16.

Jackson, P. M. (1993) 'Public service performance evaluation: a strategic perspective.' *Public Money and Management* Oct/Dec, 9–14.

Jarratt Report (1985) *Report of the Steering Committee for Studies in Universities*. London: Committee of Vice-Chancellors and Principals.

Jenkins, L., Bardsley, M., Coles, J. and Wickings, I. (1988) *How Did We*

Do? The Use of Performance Indicators in the NHS. London: CASPE Research.

Johnes, J. and Taylor, J. (1990) *Performance Indicators in Higher Education.* Buckingham: Society for Research in Higher Education and Open University.

Joint Funding Councils (1995) *The Effective Academic Library: a Framework for Evaluating the Performance of UK Academic Libraries.* Bristol: Higher Education Funding Council for England.

Joint Funding Councils' Libraries Review Group (1993) *Report.* Bristol: Higher Education Funding Council for England (Follett Report).

Jones, N. and Jordan, P. (1987) *Staff Management in Library and Information Work* (2nd ed.). Aldershot: Gower.

Jordan, P. (1992) 'Library performers: groups and individuals.' *British Journal of Academic Librarianship* **7** (3), 177–185.

Kalton, G. (1983) *Introduction to Survey Sampling.* London: Sage.

Kania, A. M. (1988) 'Academic library standards and performance measures.' *College and Research Libraries* **49** (1), 16–23.

Kantor, P. B. (1976) 'Availability analysis.' *Journal of the American Society for Information Science* **27**, 311–319.

Kantor, P. B. (1978) 'Vitality: an indirect measure of relevance.' *Collection Management* **2**, 83–95.

Kantor, P. B. (1981) 'Demand-adjusted shelf availability parameters.' *Journal of Academic Librarianship* **7**, 78–82.

Kantor, P. B. (1984) *Objective Performance Measures for Academic and Research Libraries.* Washington: Association of Research Libraries.

Kaplowitz, J. (1986) 'A pre- and post-test evaluation of the English 3 library instruction program at UCLA.' *Research Strategies* **4**, 11–17.

Kent, A. (1979) *Use of Library Materials: the University of Pittsburgh Study.* New York: Dekker.

Kesselman, M. and Watstein, S. B. (1987) 'The measurement of reference and information services.' *Journal of Academic Librarianship* **13** (1), 24–30.

Kirk, J. and Miller, M. L. (1986) *Reliability and Validity in Qualitative Research.* London: Sage.

Lancaster, F. W. (1982) 'Evaluating collections by their use.' *Collection Management* **4**, 15–43.

Lancaster, F. W. (1993) *If You Want to Evaluate Your Library* (2nd rev. ed.). London: Library Association Publishing.

Lawrence, G. S. and Oja, A. R. (1980) *The Use of General Collections at the University of California.* Sacramento: California State Department of Education.

Lawson, V. L. (1989) 'Using a computer-assisted instruction program to replace the traditional library tour: an experimental study.' *RQ* **29**, 71–79.

LeBoeuf, M. (1989) *How to Win Customers and Keep Them for Life*. New York: Berkeley Books.

Lester, R. (1979) 'Why educate the user?' *Aslib Proceedings* **31** (8), 366–380.

Lewis, S. (1986) *Output and Performance Measurement in Central Government: Progress in Departments*. London: HM Treasury.

Library Association (1982) *College Libraries: Guidelines for Professional Service and Resource Provision*. London: Library Association Publishing.

Library Association (1990) *Guidelines for College and Polytechnic Libraries* (4th ed.) London: Library Association.

Line, M. (1971) 'The information uses and needs of social scientists:an overview of INFROSS.' *Aslib Proceedings* **23** (8), 412–434.

Line, M. (1983) 'Thoughts of a non-user, non-educator.' In Fox, P. and Malley, I. (eds.) *Third International Conference on Library User Education, Edinburgh*. Loughborough: INFUSE. pp.2–9.

Line, M. (ed.) (1990) *Academic Library Management: Edited Papers of a British Council Sponsored Course, 15–27 January 1989, Birmingham*. London: Library Association.

Line, M. (1991) 'Library management styles and structures: a need to rethink?' *Journal of Librarianship and Information Science* **23** (2), 97–104.

Line, M. and Stone, S. (1982) *Library Surveys: an Introduction to the Use, Planning, Procedure and Presentation of Surveys*. London: Clive Bingley.

Lines, L. (1989) 'Performance measurement in academic libraries: a university perspective.' *British Journal of Academic Librarianship* **4** (2), 111–120.

Local Government Management Board (1994) *Performance Management and Performance Related Pay*. London: LGMB.

Local Government Training Board (1987) *Getting Closer to the Public*. Luton: Local Government Training Board.

Lockwood, D. L. (comp.) (1979) *Library Instruction: a Bibliography*. Westport, Ct.: Greenwood Press.

Long, P. (1986) *Performance Appraisal Revisited*. London: Institute of Personnel Management.

Lopez, M. D. (1983) 'The Lopez or citation technique of in-depth collection evaluation explicated.' *College and Research Libraries* **44**, 251–255.

Lovecy, I. (1994) *Convergence of Libraries and Computing Services* (Library and Information Briefings No.54). London: Library Information Technology Centre.

Lowry, C. B. (1990) 'Resource sharing or cost shifting? The unequal burden of cooperative cataloguing and interlibrary loan in network.' *College and Research Libraries* **51**, 11–19.

Lubans, J. (ed.) (1978) *Progress in Educating the Library User*. New York: Bowker.

Lund, K. and Patterson, H. (1994) *Customer Care*. London: Association of Assistant Librarians (Group of the Library Association).

MacDougall, A. (1991) 'Performance assessment: today's confusion, tomorrow's solution.' *IFLA Journal* **17** (4), 371–378.

MacDougall, A., Wheelhouse, H. and Wilson, J. M. (1990) 'Effectiveness of a local interloan system for five academic libraries: an operational research approach.' *Journal of Documentation* **46**, 353–358.

Mansbridge, J. (1986) 'Availabilty studies in libraries.' *Library and Information Science Research* **8** (4), 299–314.

Markless, S. and Streatfield, D. (1992) *Cultivating Information Skills in Further Education: Eleven Case Studies*. (Library and Information Research Report No.86). London: British Library.

Marsh, C. (1988) *Exploring Data: an Introduction to Data Analysis for Social Scientists*. Cambridge: Polity Press.

Martyn, J. and Lancaster, F. W. (1981) *Investigative Methods in Library and Information Science: an Introduction*. Arlington, Va.: Information Resources Press.

McClure, C. (1985) 'Measurement and evaluation.' In *American Library Association Yearbook*, Vol.9 1984. Chicago: American Library Association. pp.185–198.

McClure, C. R. and Hernon, P. (1983) *Improving the Quality of Reference Service for Government Publications*. Chicago: American Library Association.

McDonald, J. A. and Micikas, L. B. (1994) *Academic Libraries: the Dimensions of their Effectiveness*. Westport, Ct: Greenwood Press.

McElroy, A. R. (1989) 'Standards and guidelines in performance measurement.' *British Journal of Academic Librarianship* **4** (2), 88–98.

McKevitt, D. and Lawton, A. (eds.) (1994) *Public Sector Management: Theory, Critique and Practice*. London: Sage.

McLean, N. and Wilde, C. (1991) 'Evaluating library performance: the search for relevance.' *Australian Academic and Research Libraries* **22** (3), 198–210.

McMurdo, G. (1980) 'User satisfaction.' *New Library World* **81** (958), 83–85.

Mitchell, E. and Walters, S. (1994) *Document Delivery Services: Issues and Answers*. London: Meckler.

Mole, A (1980) 'The development of library management concerns, 1870–1950.' In Vaughan, A. (ed.) *Studies in Library Management*, Vol.6. London: Clive Bingley, pp.73–111.

Moon, P. (1993) *Appraising Your Staff*. London: Kogan Page.

Morgan, S. (1990) Self-instruction techniques in user education: workbook versus lecture. *Education Libraries Journal* **33** (1), 14–39.

Morgan, S. (1992) *Performance Assessment in Academic Libraries*. Unpublished MBA thesis. Open University.

Morgan, S. (1993) 'Performance assessment in higher education libraries.' *Library Management* **14** (5), 35–42.

Morley, M. and Woodward, H. (eds.) (1993) *Taming the Electronic Jungle: Electronic Information: the Collection Management Issues*. Papers presented at a conference organized by the National Acquisitions Group and the UK Serials Group at Market Bosworth, Leicestershire, May 1993. Leeds: NAG and UKSG.

Morrison, M. (1991) *Information Skills in Further Education: the Development Report* (British Library Research and Development Report 6058). London: British Library.

Morrison, M. and Markless, S. (1992) *Enhancing Information Skills in Further Education: Some Strategies for Senior Managers, Lecturers and Librarians*. London: British Library.

Morse, P. (1968) *Library Effectiveness: a Systems Approach*. Cambridge, Mass.: MIT Press.

Moser, C. A. and Kalton, G. (1971) *Survey Methods in Social Investigation* (2nd ed.) London: Heinemann.

Myers, M. J. and Jirjees, J. M. (1983) *The Accuracy of Telephone Reference/Information Services in Academic Libraries*. Metuchen, N.J.: Scarecrow Press.

Nichols, J. (1993) 'Library orientation: a workable alternative reworked.' *Library Review* **42** (7), 5–14.

Nisonger, T. E. (1992) *Collection Evaluation in Academic Libraries: a Literature Guide and Annotated Bibliography*. Englewood, Colo.: Libraries Unlimited.

Noon, P. (1991) 'Librarians as managers:a different set of skills?' *Library Management* **12** (5), 4–12.

Olson, L. M. (1984) 'Reference service evaluation in medium-sized academic libraries: a model.' *Journal of Academic Librarianship* **9** (6), 322–329.

Olszak, L. (1991) 'Mistakes and failures at the reference desk.' *RQ* **31** (1), 39–49.

Open University (1991) *B887 Managing Public Services*. Milton Keynes: Open University Press.

Oppenheim, A. N. (1992) *Questionnaire Design, Interviewing and Attitude Measurement*. London: Pinter.

Orr, R. H. (1973) 'Measuring the goodness of library services: a general framework for considering quantitative measures.' *Journal of Documentation* **29** (3), 315–332.

Pack, P. (ed.) (1994) *Funding and Performance: Income, Expenditure and Performance After Incorporation: Implications for College Libraries and Learning Resources*. Thirsk: Underhill Press.

Pack, P. J. and Pack, F. M. (1988) *Colleges, Learning and Libraries: the Future*. London: Clive Bingley.

Parlett, M. and Hamilton, D. (1976) 'Evaluation as illumination.' In Tawney, D. (ed.) *Curriculum Evaluation Today: Trends and Implications*. London: Macmillan for Schools Council. pp. 84–101.

Patton, M. Q. (1990) *Qualitative Evaluation Methods* (2nd ed.). London: Sage.

Perkins, R. (1965) *The Prospective Teacher's Knowledge of Library Fundamentals*. Metuchen, N.J.: Scarecrow Press.

Peters, T. J. and Waterman, R. H. (1982) *In Search of Excellence: Lessons from America's Best Run Companies*. New York: Harper and Row.

Pollitt, C. (1986) 'Beyond the managerial model: the case for broadening performance assessment in government and the public services.' *Financial Accountability and Management* **2** (3), Autumn 155–170.

Pollitt, C. (1988) 'Bringing consumers into performance measurement: concepts, consequences and constraints.' *Policy and Politics* **16** (2), 77–87.

Pollitt, C. (1993) *Managerialism and the Public Services: Cuts or Cultural Change in the 1990s?* (2nd ed.). Oxford: Blackwell.

Pollitt, C. and Harrison, S. (1992) *Handbook of Public Services Management*. Oxford: Blackwell.

Powell, R. R. (1984) 'Reference effectiveness:a review of research.' *Library and Information Science Research* **6** (1), 3–19.

Powell, R. R. (1985) *Basic Research Methods for Librarians*. Norwood, N.J.: Ablex Publishing.

Powell, R. R. (1988) *The Relationship of Library User Studies to Performance Measures: a Review of the Literature* (Occasional Paper No.181). Illinois: University of Illinois Graduate School of Library and Information Science.

Powell, R. R. (1992) 'Impact assessment of university libraries: a consideration of issues and research methodologies.' *Library and Information Science Review* **14** (3), 245–257.

Revill, D. H. (1987) 'Availability as a performance measure for academic libraries.' *Journal of Librarianship* **19** (1), 14–30.

Revill, D. H. (1988) 'An availability survey in cooperation with a School of Librarianship and Information Studies.' *Library Review* **37** (1), 17–34.

Revill, D. H. (1991) 'Availability.' In Revill, D. H. (ed.). *Working Papers in Management Issues: In-house Research*. Brighton: COPOL. pp.15–21.

Reynolds, R. (1970) *A Selective Bibliography on Measurement in Library and Information Services*. London: Aslib.

Richard, S. (1992) 'Library use of performance indicators.' *Library Review* **41** (6), 22–36.

Rizzo, J. R. (1980) *Management for Librarians: Fundamentals and Issues*. Westport, Conn: Greenwood.

Robson, C. (1993) *Real World Research: a Resource for Social Scientists and Practitioner-Researchers.* Oxford: Blackwell.

Roes, H. and Dijkstra, J. (1994) 'Ariadne: the next generation of electronic document delivery systems.' *The Electronic Library* **12** (1), 13–19.

Rogers, S. (1990) *Performance Management in Local Government.* Harlow: Longman.

Rouse, J. (1993) 'Resource and performance management in public service organizations.' In Isaac-Henry, K., Painter, C. and Barnes, C. (eds.) *Management in the Public Sector.* London: Chapman and Hall. pp.59- 76.

Rowley, J. (1994) 'Revolution in current awareness services.' *Journal of Librarianship and Information Science* **26** (1), 7–14.

St.Clair, G. (1993) *Customer Service in the Information Environment.* London: Bowker Saur.

Sallis, E. (1990) *The National Quality Survey* (Mendip Paper No. 9). Bristol: Further Education Staff College.

Salter, E. (1992) *The Evaluation of Library Service Effectiveness With Particular Reference to FE Libraries.* Unpublished MLib thesis. University College of Wales, Aberystwyth.

Salter, E. (1993) 'How good is the library provision in FE colleges?' *Library Association Record* **95** (6), 348–349.

Salter, E. (1994) 'Quality performance indicators in further education college libraries.' In Pack, P. (ed.) *Funding and Performance.* Thirsk: Underhill Press. pp.29–37.

SCONUL (1992) *Performance Indicators for University Libraries: a Practical Guide.* London: SCONUL.

Scriven, M. (1967) 'The methodology of evaluation.' In Tyler, R. W., Gagne, R. M. and Scriven, M. (eds.) *Perspectives of Curriculum Evaluation.* Chicago: Rand McNally.

Selegean, J. C., Thomas, M. L. and Richman, M. L. (1983) 'Long-range effectiveness of library use instruction.' *College and Research Libraries* **44** (6), 476–480.

Seymour, C. A. and Schofield, J. L. (1973) 'Measuring reader failure at the catalogue.' *Library Resources and Technical Services* **17** (1), 6–24.

Shapiro, B. J. (1992) 'Access and performance measures in research libraries in the 1990s.' *Journal of Library Administration* **15** (3/4), 49–66.

Shaw, W. M. (1980) 'Longitudinal studies of book availability.' In *Library Effectiveness: a State of the Art.* Chicago: American Library Association. pp.338–349.

Shipman, M. (1988) *The Limitations of Social Research* (3rd ed.). London: Longman.

Slater, M. (1989) *Information Needs of Social Scientists: a Study by Desk Research and Interview* (British Library Research Paper No.60). London: British Library.

Slater, M. (ed.) (1990) *Research Methods in Library and Information Studies*. London: Library Association Publishing.

Slote, S. J. (1898) *Weeding Library Collections* (3rd ed.). Littleton, Colo.: Libraries Unlimited.

Smith, H. W. (1975) *Strategies of Social Research: the Methodological Imagination*. London: Prentice-Hall.

Smith, I. (1994) *Meeting Customer Needs*. Oxford: Butterworth-Heinemann.

Stone, S. and Harris, C. (1984) *CRUS Guide 1.Designing a User Study: General Research Design*. Sheffield: Centre for Research on User Studies.

Tiefel, V. (1989) 'Evaluating a library user education program: a decade of experience.' *College and Research Libraries* **50**, 249–259.

Town, S. (1995) *Benchmarking in Libraries: a report on the Royal Military College Shrivenham Project including a benchmarking exercise involving eighteen academic libraries*. Cranfield University: RMCS Information Services Report No.12.

Trow, M. (1977) 'Methodological problems in the evaluation of innovation.' In Caro, F. G. (ed.) *Readings in Evaluation Research*. London: Russell Sage Foundation. pp.81–94.

Trueswell, R. W. (1964) 'Two characteristics of circulation and their effects on the implementation of mechanized circulation control systems.' *College and Research Libraries* **25**, 285–291.

Trueswell, R. W. (1965) 'A quantitative measure of user circulation requirements and its possible effect on stack thinning and multiple copy determination.' *American Documentation* **16**, 20–25.

Trueswell, R. W. (1966) 'Determining the optimal number for volumes for a library's core collection.' *Libri* **16**, 49–60.

Trueswell, R. W. (1969) 'User circulation satisfaction vs. size of holdings at three academic libraries.' *College and Research Libraries* **30**, 204–213.

Universities Funding Council (1992) *Research Assessment Exercise, 1992: the outcome*. (Circular 26/92) Bristol: UFC.

Urquhart, J. A. and Schofield, J. L. (1971) 'Measuring readers' failure at the shelf.' *Journal of Documentation* **27** (4), 273–286.

Utley, A. (1994) 'Most FE colleges reject BS5750 quality standard.' *Times Higher Education Supplement* No.1132 (22 July).

Van House, N. (1989) 'Output measures in libraries.' *Library Trends* **38** (2), 268–279.

Van House, N., Weil, B. T. and McClure, C. R. (1990) *Measuring Academic Library Performance: a Practical Approach*. Chicago: American Library Association.

Verrill, P. E. (1993) 'Performance appraisal for the 1990s:managerial threat or professional right?' *British Journal of Academic Librarianship* **8** (2), 98–112.

Von Seggern, M. (1987) 'Assessment of reference services.' *RQ* **26** (4), 487–496.

Wainwright, E. J. and Dean, J. E. (1976) *Measures of Adequacy for Library Collections in Australian Colleges of Advanced Education: Report of a Research Project Conducted on Behalf of the Commission on Advanced Education:* Vol.2. Perth: Western Australia Institute of Technology.

Waldhart, T. J. (1985) 'Performance evaluation of interlibrary loan in the United States: a review of research.' *Library and Information Science* **7**, 313–331.

Webb, E. J. (1966) *Unobtrusive Measures: Non-reactive Research in the Social Sciences.* Chicago: Rand McNally.

Werking, R. H. (1980) 'Evaluating bibliographic education:a review and critique.' *Library Trends* **29** (1), 153–172.

Wessel, C. J. (1968) 'Criteria for evaluating technical library effectiveness.' *Aslib Proceedings* **20** (11), 455–481.

White, M. D. (1985) 'Evaluation of the reference interview.' *RQ* **25** (1), 76–84.

Whitlatch, J. B. (1989) 'Unobtrusive studies and the quality of academic library reference services.' *College and Research Libraries* **50** (2), 181–94.

Whitlatch, J. B. and Kieffer, K. (1978) Service at San Jose State University: survey of document availability. *Journal of Academic Librarianship* **4**, 196–199.

Whittaker, K. (1993) *The Basics of Library-Based Services.* London: Library Association Publishing.

Willemse, J. (1993) 'Improving interlending through goal setting and performance measurement.' *Interlending and Document Supply* **21** (1), 13–17.

Williams, R. (1987) 'An unobtrusive survey of academic library reference services.' *Library and Information Research News* **10** (37/38), 12–40.

Winkworth, I. (1990) 'Performance indicators for polytechnic libraries.' *Library Review* **39** (5), 23–41.

Winkworth, I. (1991) 'Performance measurement and performance indicators.' In Jenkins, C. and Morley, M. (eds.) *Collection Management in Academic Libraries.* Aldershot: Gower. pp.57–93.

Winkworth, I. (1993) 'Libraries and quality: performance indicators.' In McElroy, A. R. (ed.) *Quality Matters: Proceedings of the Annual COFHE Study Conference, Canterbury, 13–16 April 1992.* London: Library Association (COFHE Group). pp.31–44.

Woodward, H. (1994) 'The impact of electronic information on serials collection management.' *Serials* **7** (1) 29–36.

Yeates, J. D. (1990) *Performance Appraisal: a Guide for Design and Implementation* (IMS Report No.188). Brighton: Institute of Manpower Studies.

Index